How to Win at Job Hunting

Copyright © Iain Maitland 1989

First published in Great Britain by
Business Books Limited
An Imprint of Century Hutchinson Limited
62–65 Chandos Place, London WC2N 4NW

Century Hutchinson Australia (Pty) Limited
89–91 Albion Street, Surry Hills,
New South Wales 2010, Australia

Century Hutchinson New Zealand Limited
PO Box 40–086, 32–34 View Road, Glenfield,
Auckland 10, New Zealand

Century Hutchinson South Africa (Pty) Limited
PO Box 337, Bergvlei 2012, South Africa

Phototypeset by Input Typesetting Ltd, London

British Library Cataloguing in Publication Data

Maitland, Iain
  How to win at jobhunting
  1. Jobhunting. Manuals
  I. Title
  650.1'4

  ISBN 0–09–174079–7

Printed in Great Britain by
Cox & Wyman Ltd, Reading

How to Win at Job Hunting

Iain Maitland

Business Books

ACKNOWLEDGMENTS

I wish to thank the following people who supplied information on recruitment and selection procedures: Vivien Charters at Imperial Chemical Industries Plc, Elly Slocock at Wimpy International, the Recruiting Officer and K. Drinkwater at the Metropolitan Police Office Cadet Selection Centre. Their kind and generous assistance is greatly appreciated.

I also wish to thank Imperial Chemical Industries Plc, Wimpy International and the Metropolitan Police for allowing me to reproduce various documents within the text.

May I also thank Tim Cornford at NFER–Nelson Publishing Company Ltd for his assistance concerning the 7-point plan mentioned in the text.

Finally, my special thanks to my wife, Tracey, for her constant help.

Iain Maitland

CONTENTS

Chapter Five: Using the Telephone

Chapter Six: Preparing for the Interview

Chapter Seven: The Interview

CHAPTER ONE

READY, STEADY . . . GO?

WHAT DO YOU WANT TO DO?

WHAT CAN YOU OFFER AN EMPLOYER?

WHERE TO FIND VACANCIES

IS THIS THE JOB FOR YOU?

CHAPTER ONE

READY, STEADY . . . GO?

If you're reading this book you should have already decided on the type of job or career you want.

Nevertheless you may still be uncertain about what you want to do. You may, for example, have a vague idea that you want to be a 'writer' because you've always enjoyed reading and were good at English at school. What type of writer though and where do you start? Should you go to university to obtain a degree in English Literature? Would that help you to succeed? Perhaps you should go to college and obtain a diploma in journalism. What college though and what sort of courses do they offer exactly? Alternatively, should you apply for a job as a trainee reporter on your local paper or try to work on a freelance basis selling articles to national newspapers and magazines?

WHAT DO YOU WANT TO DO?

You cannot start job hunting if you haven't yet decided what you want to do. You must have a firm long-term ambition that you can work towards. There are many different routes you can take to achieve that ambition, but every job you apply for should be a specific step in the right direction. Don't just apply for a job because 'the money's good'. It may be now, but what will it be like in ten years time? Don't take a job because 'it's

3

all there is'. Look to the future. Don't get stuck in a dead end job.

If you are uncertain as to what you want to do or whether a particular job is a step in the right direction then, clearly, a book on job hunting cannot really help you. There are a number of sources of help and advice though which you should turn to before reading this book.

Your school, college or university should have a counselling and careers service. Careers officers, or 'student counsellors', will be available to advise you on many subjects including future careers. They will be able to help you choose a suitable career and discuss with you the particular qualifications and experience you will need to have in order to succeed.

Similarly, there are many independent, professional 'careers consultants' who may help you for an appropriate fee. They will assess you in many different areas (refer to 'What Can You Offer An Employer? page 5) and will suggest the type of career that might suit you. They will also be able to assist you generally in job hunting. You will find the names and addresses of such consultants in your local Yellow Pages. Telephone them to enquire exactly what they offer and at what price. Ask if you might be able to contact one or two 'satisfied customers'. What did they think of the service? Try to obtain a personal recommendation before you part with any money.

You should also read as many books on 'Careers' as you can. Most libraries will have a good selection of careers encyclopaedias and books. A list of recommended ones is included in the bibliography on page 176.

If you are thinking of entering a particular trade or profession then you should also read the appropriate *Careers in . . .* booklets published by Kogan Page. These are short guides written especially for school and college leavers. They give general information on the type of jobs available within a particular field and also provide details on necessary qualifications and courses available. A full list is given in the bibliography. Obtain a copy of the appropriate title from your local bookshop or library, or contact Kogan Page at 120 Pentonville Road, London N1 9JN.

Similarly, if you are considering, for example, a career in

accountancy or surveying, then you should get in touch with the appropriate trade or professional association. They may offer helpful advice and information. Visit you local library and look in *The Directory of British Associations*. Alternatively, why not get in touch with a local accountant or surveyor who may put you in touch. They may also offer you help and advice themselves.

WHAT CAN YOU OFFER AN EMPLOYER?

Before you start job hunting you must consider what you have to offer an employer. You need to identify your own strengths and weaknesses.

Professor Alec Rodger at the National Institute of Industrial Psychology has devised an excellent Seven Point Plan which many employers use to analyse the type of applicant they require to fill a vacancy. They may also use this plan to assess applicants during an interview.

You too can use the plan to analyse yourself:

Physical Make Up

Consider, for example:

- Age
- Appearance
- Speech
- Health
- Physique

Look at each of these areas in turn. Are you strong in each one? For example, think about your appearance. Is this a strength or a weakness? What would an employer think? If it is a weakness how can you improve it?

Similarly, consider your speech. Is it an asset or a handicap?

Think about it in relation to the type of job you want. A 'posh' voice may be an asset in one job but a handicap in another.

Attainments

Consider, for example:

- Academic Qualifications
- Training
- Experience
- Skills
- Knowledge

Judge yourself under these headings. Do you, for example, have good qualifications and suitable training for the type of job you want? Do you have any experience to offer an employer? If not, perhaps you have some special skills or knowledge instead. Again, if any of these areas could be considered as weaknesses, how could they become strengths? Could you, for example, obtain further qualifications by going to evening classes or returning to college?

Intelligence

How intelligent are you? Can you, for example, work out and easily solve problems? Can you understand ideas expressed in different ways? Can you think and reason for yourself? Have you got common sense? What type of intelligence do you need for a particular job? Is it, for example, a job where you will have to solve different problems quickly without help? Could you cope?

Aptitudes

Consider, for example these aptitudes:

- Mechanical
- Manual

- Numerical
- Verbal

What special aptitudes do you have? Are you good with your hands or with figures? Are you a good talker? Do these strengths match up to the requirements of your chosen job? There is obviously little point in pursuing a career in accountancy if you do not have an aptitude for figures. There is, similarly, little point in pursuing a job as a car mechanic if you do not have a mechanical aptitude.

Interests

Consider, for example, the following interests:

- Physical
- Social
- Artistic
- Intellectual

What sort of interests do you have? Do you enjoy sports? Do you enjoy socialising and going to discos and night clubs? Perhaps you have artistic interests such as painting, drawing or writing? You may also enjoy intellectual hobbies such as chess or bridge. Think about your hobbies. Could they help you when you start job hunting?

Disposition

What are you like as a person? Are you calm or excitable? Dependable and reliable or rather erratic? Are you self-motivated and ambitious? A leader or a follower? A team member or an individual? Think about your disposition. What are your strengths and weaknesses? How can you turn your weaknesses to strengths?

Circumstances

Think about your personal circumstances and how they could affect you when you start job hunting. Do you, for example, have a car, motorcycle or bicycle? Are you mobile? This could obviously be an advantage to you. Think about your family circumstances. Do you, for example, have elderly parents to care for? This could, of course, be a disadvantage. You may not, perhaps, be able to re-locate for promotion.

Think about yourself carefully before you apply for any job. Make sure you know what your strengths are. You will need to tell the employer what they are and how they would help you to do the job well. It is, however, as important that you recognise your weaknesses. No-one is perfect. Pinpoint the weaker areas and try to eliminate them.

WHERE TO FIND VACANCIES

There are many different ways you can find out about job vacancies. Try them all. Do not let any potentially suitable job pass by without applying for it. Even if you are unsuccessful, the experience will be of benefit. Practice makes perfect. The more jobs you apply for the better you will get and the quicker you may succeed.

Consider the following:

Contacts

Friends, relatives and business acquaintances can all help you. Many jobs are filled through 'word of mouth'. They are never advertised. A vacancy arises and the employer immediately knows someone suitable who can take over. Make sure that someone is you.

Tell your contacts what you want to do and what you can

offer. Let them be extra eyes and ears for you. Get in touch with them regularly to remind them you're still job hunting.

Careers Office

The careers officer will not only help you to decide what you want to do but may also have details of jobs available. Towards the end of the school year many local employers will contact schools and colleges with details of current or forthcoming vacancies. Tell the careers officer what you want and speak to him or her regularly.

Job Centres

You must visit job centres every day. Be there when the door opens. Be first to see the vacancy. Be first to apply. Talk to the staff. They can often help. They may know of imminent vacancies. They can offer you advice about job hunting and job conditions. They can also offer advice about Government training schemes and other opportunities currently available.

Employment Agencies

Look through the local Yellow Pages and contact all the employment agencies in your area. They may help. High-street employment agencies are usually retained by employers to advertise for staff and weed out unsuitable applicants before a shortlist is forwarded to the employer to arrange interviews. Normally the employer, rather than the applicant, pays a fee, but do check this out before you sign anything.

Direct Approach

You should always approach potential employers regularly even if no vacancy appears available. A speculative approach can often work. You may be lucky. Your letter may arrive on an employer's desk at the time when he is thinking of creating a new job or employee is resigning, retiring or being promoted.

Look through reference books and Yellow Pages in your local library to obtain a list of potential employers and then 'phone or write to them. Listen to the radio, read newspapers and planning applications regularly. If a new business is opening, re-locating, manufacturing a new product, offering a new service or changing staff, then you should write to them too. There may be a vacancy.

The Media

Listen to the radio. Many local radio stations have regular 'job search' features. Ring the radio station to find out when these will be broadcast. Why not try to establish a friendly relationship with the staff? Perhaps you can find out about vacancies before others do.

Read newspapers every day. Most national newspapers have job sections and also have special employment features on a regular basis. At the time of writing, for example, the *Daily Express* has an 'Employment Plus' feature every Tuesday. Vacancies are advertised and the feature is always full of good tips. Some newspapers have specific groups of advertisements on particular days. For example, at the time of writing *The Guardian* advertises media vacancies every Monday.

You should also read local and free newspapers if you are seeking work just in your own area. Contact the newspaper to see which day most advertisements are published. Be first to buy it. Be first to reply.

Trade Magazines

Many trade magazines carry job advertisements. Once you know the trade or profession you want to enter, you should, as previously indicated, contact the trade association for information. They will also tell you if the trade has its own magazine and, if so, who publishes it. Subscribe to it. Not only will the magazine often have details of vacancies, but it will be full of other news and information you can use in the job hunting process.

Self-Promotion

Why not take out a small advertisement in a newspaper or magazine yourself? Briefly state what you want and what you have to offer. It may work. It shows initiative which is a quality most employers look for in an employee.

IS THIS JOB FOR YOU?

You now know what you want to do. You have a long-term ambition. You also know what you have to offer an employer. You know where you can find vacancies.

You now want to find out as much as you can about a job before you apply. You need to know that you are suitable and that you really want it. You should, if appropriate, study the job advertisement. For example:

> '. . . We currently have a vacancy for an organiser in our knitting department. The job involves the control and quality of production via outworkers. The successful applicant must have a working knowledge of machine knitting, clerical experience and a clean driving licence. A sense of humour would also be an asset. Apply . . .'

If you study this advertisement you can discover if you are suitable for the job and if it is what you want to do. The suitable applicant *must* have knowledge of machine knitting, clerical experience and a clean driving licence. If you do not, then you are clearly unsuitable and should not apply. Your application would automatically be discarded when the employer saw you did not fulfil his basic requirements.

If you do fulfil the initial requirements set by the employer, read the advertisement again. There are always 'hidden' requirements in the advertisement which you will need to satisfy if you want the job. Analyse these requirements. They will also help you to decide if you really want the job.

For example, for this job you would need to be an 'organiser'. Are you a good organiser? You would be responsible for 'the control and quality of production via outworkers'. Can you chivvy along slow workers? Can you satisfy those workers who always want more work? What if there is no work available: could you still keep them happy? How would you deal with outworkers who produced sub-standard work? Do you enjoy meeting and dealing with people? Do you also enjoy driving? This is obviously part of the job too. The advertisement also states that a sense of humour would be an asset. Why? The last occupant was probably driven mad by the outworkers! Can you fulfil all these 'hidden' requirements and, on reflection, is this what you want to do?

> '. . . A vacancy exists for a trainee horticultural manager at our Thretford nursery. The successful applicant will be responsible for maintaining and selling outdoor and indoor plants to the public. Applicants must be over 21 and should have suitable qualifications. Apply . . .'

Are you suitable for this job? The basic requirements are that you must firstly be over 21. There may or may not be a good reason for this but the advertisement states 'must'. You will not, therefore, succeed if you are below that age. In addition, you should have 'suitable qualifications'. The word 'should' is important. If the advertisement said 'you must have suitable qualifications' then, unless you had relevant certificates or diplomas, your application would fail. By writing 'should' the advertiser indicates that qualifications would certainly be preferable but are not necessarily essential. The applicant with, for example, suitable experience instead may be considered.

When you read advertisements, do read them carefully. If

applicants 'must' have certain qualities then, to succeed, you must obviously have them. If you 'should' have certain qualities then it is not a necessity and your application would be considered if you had other qualities to offer.

Read the advertisement for a trainee horticultural manager again for those 'hidden' requirements. What other qualities must you have to get the job? Again, from these, you can judge if you really want the job. You are a 'trainee manager'. You are therefore going to be working as part of a team. Are you a team person or an individual? A trainee manager is, of course, being groomed to be a manager. Is that what you want? Do you want responsibility? You will also have to 'maintain and sell outdoor and indoor plants to the public'. Do you want to work outdoors, especially in winter? Do you want to sell? Are you a good salesman? Again, do you match these 'hidden' requirements and is this what you really want to do? Is it a step in the right direction?

You also need to know how to apply for the job. This is important. An employer will not be impressed if you appear on his doorstep expecting an interview when the advertisement stated you should apply for an application form.

The advertisement could state, for example:

'Please contact Brenda Hinton for an application form on (0446) 92476.'

or

'Write, for an application form, to. . . .'

Follow the instructions. If you're expected to complete an application form then, regardless of your personal preferences, you must do it. Refer to chapter two on 'Application Forms'.

Alternatively, the advertisement may state:

'Apply with a full C.V. to . . . .'

or

'Applications in writing only with a C.V. . . . .'

13

or

'Apply in writing with a full C.V. and quote reference ZP432 . . .'

Similarly you must apply with a curriculum vitae if this is indicated. These are looked at in more detail in Chapter Three: 'Curricula Vitae', page 75.

An advertisement might also state:

'Please write with full details to . . .'

or

'Write, with full career details, to . . .'

or

'Apply in writing to . . .'

or

'Please apply in writing with details of age, qualifications and experience . . .'

In these circumstances you have a choice. You can send in a C.V. with a supporting letter or alternatively just send in a letter of application. Both supporting letters and letters of application are dealt with in Chapter Four: 'Writing Letters'.

Alternatively, an advertisement might state:

'Apply by telephoning . . .'

or

'Please contact Geoffrey Lonsdale for an informal chat on . . .'

You may, of course, be asked to telephone the company. In many ways you are therefore cutting through much of the job hunting process and could be 'interviewed' immediately. The employer may prefer to obtain a shortlist for a final 'face to face' interview by talking to applicants on the telephone rather than reading application forms, C.V's or letters. Refer to Chapter Five: 'Using the Telephone', and Chapter Seven: 'The Interview'.

Some advertisements will conclude with:

'For further information contact . . .'

or

'For more details telephone or write to . . .'

Before you apply for any job it is, of course, important that you obtain as much information as you can about both the job and indeed the organisation you could be working for. You can, as you have seen, obtain some information from studying the advertisement. Many will be very detailed about the employer's requirements and pay, terms and conditions. Some will also supply information about the company. Nevertheless, studying the advertisement alone is often insufficient to fully judge whether you're suitable or if you even want the job.

Always contact the organisation before you apply, even if the advertisement does not specifically state 'for further information contact..' or 'for more details telephone or write to..'. Few organisations would object to a genuine, interested enquiry. Obtain any literature you can about the company to find out more about it. Do you really want to work for them? (You should also refer to the section entitled 'Researching the Organisation' on page 130 in Chapter Six: 'Preparing for the Interview'.)

There are also some job-related documents you might be able to obtain from the company. When an organisation decides to employ staff, it will normally analyse the job in order to decide on the type of person it needs to fill it. The documents it produces can be very helpful to you.

A 'job description' is often drawn up by an employer. It will usually be available to applicants on request or may even be

sent out automatically with an application form. A job description details the main purpose and tasks of the job. Although
there is no set way of compiling a job description it will normally detail the following:

- Job Title
- Job Title of the Job Holder's Superior
- Job Titles of the Job Holder's Subordinates
- Purpose of the Job
- Tasks of the Job

Here is a simple example of a job description.

JOB DESCRIPTION

Job Title:	Office Junior
Responsible to:	Office Manageress
Responsible for:	N/A
Purpose of Job:	To complete clerical work as required.
Tasks:	To record, distribute and file copies of incoming mail.
	To record, file copies and post outgoing mail.
	To type correspondence when required.
	To run general errands as required.
	To maintain stocks of office stationery.

You should, if possible, always try to obtain a job description
for every job you apply for. It will help you to understand
what the job involves and to decide whether you really want
it.

Some organisations will also produce a job specification. This
considers the main tasks indicated within the job description
and, taking each individual task in turn, will look at the knowledge and skills required to do that particular task well.
Obviously if the job involves many varied tasks then the job
specification may be quite lengthy.

As with a job description layout, style and content may vary
considerably but an extract from an office job specification may
appear as follows:

JOB SPECIFICATION

TASK	KNOWLEDGE REQUIRED	SKILLS REQUIRED
To answer the telephone, pass on and record messages.	Of the company's telephone system.	Ability to communicate verbally well with different types of people.
	Of the company's organisational structure.	Ability to correctly interpret and transmit messages.
	Of telephone documentation (memo's etc . . .) and company's communication network.	Ability to communicate well in writing (neat handwriting, correct spelling etc)

If you cannot obtain a job specification for the job you are applying for, you should nevertheless think about the knowledge and skills you think would be required. Do you have them?

Following on from this you may be able to obtain a person, or 'personnel', specification. This considers the job specification and then details the type of person required. Professor Alec Rodgers Seven Point Plan is widely used as the basis for a personnel specification. It considers:

- Physical Make Up
- Attainments
- Intelligence
- Aptitudes
- Interests
- Disposition
- Circumstances

An example of a personnel specification for an office junior may be:

17

PERSONNEL SPECIFICATION

PHYSICAL MAKE UP	– Neat and tidy appearance
	– Well spoken
	– Pleasant manner
	– Good health
ATTAINMENTS	– GCSE passes in English Language and Mathematics
	– Ability to type
	– Ability to operate office machinery
	– Previous office experience (if possible)
INTELLIGENCE	– Common sense
	– Quick to adapt to situations
APTITUDES	– Must show manual aptitude (for operating office machinery).
	– Must show verbal aptitude (for using the telephone).
INTERESTS	– Must show social interests as the job involves contact with the public, customers and inter-relating with other staff.
DISPOSITION	– Calm
	– Reliable
	– Self-motivated
CIRCUMSTANCES	– Must have no personal or domestic problems that may affect performance or work rate.

If you are fortunate enough to see a personnel specification, compare it to the notes you drew up under the same headings in 'What Can You Offer an Employer?' Is it similar? It should be if this is the right job for you!

You must, of course, remember that when you apply for these various documents that each organisation is different. Some will not produce any of these documents at all. They may feel they are unnecessary. Others may produce perhaps one document which is an amalgamation of all three. Expect the unexpected! The important fact is that you simply obtain further information about the job in whatever form it is available.

From the advertisement, job description and specifications you should now know whether or not you are suitable and whether you want the job. You also know, of course, how you are expected to apply.

Before you now start job hunting in earnest there are a few final points to consider.

Be industrious: Job hunting is a full time job. Treat it as such. Don't let yourself fall into bad habits such as lying in bed all morning and thinking you'll do it later. By then the job will have gone.

Be first: See or hear the job advert first. Get the information you need before anyone else. Get your application in as quickly as you can. Always be 'on the ball'.

Be organised: Get into a regular daily habit of, perhaps, visiting the job centre first, then checking the day's papers before writing a number of speculative letters. Set up a job file. Keep all the job details and copies of any letters you send. You may need to refer to them again. You may, for example, receive a reply to a speculative letter suggesting you write again in six months. Keep it. In six month's time you'll have a record of the person you should write to within the company.

Be flexible: Don't limit yourself too much to a particular job, area or salary. The job may not be perfect but it could still be a step in the right direction. Always be flexible about your applications too. Match your application to the specific job. Read all those documents again. Remember that they are drawn up to help the company find the ideal applicant. The company will only be able to decide if you are ideal if you tell them and prove it by matching each of your strengths to each of their requirements.

CHAPTER TWO

APPLICATION FORMS

OBTAINING AN APPLICATION FORM

PREPARATION

COMPLETING AN APPLICATION FORM

CHAPTER TWO

APPLICATION FORMS

Many job advertisements will ask you to write in or telephone for an application form.

If you decide to write to the company, do it immediately and send it today by first class post. You must be quick to reply. It shows enthusiasm. It is not unknown for some employers to automatically eliminate those applicants who reply 'late' or by second class post. It is unfair, but for vacancies where there are dozens (sometimes hundreds) of replies the employer must eliminate the majority in some way. He cannot, after all, interview every applicant. So be quick and be seen to be quick. Apply on the day the advertisement comes out. If you don't see or hear of it until a few days later you may find it is no longer worth applying for.

OBTAINING AN APPLICATION FORM

Keep your letter short and concise. At this stage you are not trying to sell yourself but are simply requesting an application form. Here is an example of this type of letter:

Dear Sir,
re: Vacancy for Trainee Manager (TM 37)
Would you please forward an application form for the above vacancy as advertised in today's 'Daily Echo'. I would also

appreciate any further information such as a job description, specification or company literature.

I enclose a stamped addressed envelope for your convenience.

Yours faithfully

Michael James

Michael James

Enc.

It is important that you make it absolutely clear which vacancy
you will be applying for. Quote any reference number given in
the advertisement or, alternatively, indicate which one it is by
stating, for example, '. . . as advertised in today's 'Daily Echo'.
Remember it is not unusual (especially in large organisations)
for several vacancies to exist at the same time. Many applicants
do not indicate the vacancy they wish to fill and so are sent the
wrong form or details.

You must, of course, also seek to obtain further information
about the job or organisation. Ask for it. If you can obtain a
job description or specifications it will help you to match up
your qualities to those the employer is looking for. Ask for
company literature too. Find out as much about the organisation
as you can. It may help. For example, if the company is very
proud of its sports teams and comments on its success in a
brochure, then it would be sensible to highlight your sporting
interests on the application form. Similarly, if the company
boasts about the number of employees who pass exams on day
release courses, then you should also indicate an interest in this.
Be smart. Give them what they want to read.

You should always enclose a stamped addressed envelope. It
shows courtesy. It can also help you. It makes it that little bit
easier for the secretary or clerk to act immediately. He or she
doesn't have to rummage round for an envelope and then write
or type your name and address on it. The envelope is there,
ready and waiting, in their hand.

If you've asked (as you should) for company literature, do
remember that some brochures will not fold up and fit into a
standard sized business envelope. Send a large A4 manilla en-

velope which should hold most literature. Again, it encourages a good, quick response. Always attach first class stamps as well for a speedy reply. (Letters are dealt with in more detail in Chapter Four : Writing Letters.)

Alternatively, of course, you can telephone for an application form. The same basic rules apply whether you write or telephone. Be quick. Do it now. Be brief. At this stage, your enquiry will probably be dealt with by a secretary or a clerk in the personnel department. They are not interested in listening to or reading about your qualifications, experience or abilities, so don't tell them. (Read Chapter Five : Using the Telephone, before telephoning for an application form.)

An alternative to ringing or writing is to personally go to the company and collect the application form. If you ring or write it will often take three or four days before the application form is back on the right desk. If you're on the ball you will see the advert in the morning, be at the company collecting the application form at lunchtime and have the completed form back at the company and on the right desk by mid-afternoon. If you really want the job that is the way to succeed. You will be at the head of the queue and the employer will already have marked you out as enthusiastic, keen and quick off the mark.

PREPARATION

Once you have the application form it is, as indicated, important that you return it quickly. To do this you must be well prepared and know how to complete it in a way which will show you in the best light. There are a number of points to consider.

You must, firstly, complete the actual application form. It is not enough just to write 'See the attached C.V.' or 'Refer to the enclosed letter' across it as many applicants do. Such an application will often be automatically discarded. The employer wants a set of matching forms which he or she can compare easily.

It is important to remember that an application form is used to weed out unsuitable applicants and to shortlist perhaps a dozen who are worth interviewing. An employer will quickly reduce perhaps a hundred or more applicants to just twelve by judging each application by a number of criteria. (See 'Is this the Job for You?' in Chapter One, page 11.)

For example, he may halve the number of applicants by eliminating all those who have less than four 'O' levels and halve the remainder again by eliminating those with no previous experience. Of course, such a system of elimination can be unfair. The applicant with less than four 'O' levels and no experience may have had all the other qualities the employer was looking for. However, the initial list of applicants has to be reduced in some way. The employer does not want to interview perhaps a hundred people for just one job.

To make this weeding out process work quickly he or she will want, as indicated, a matching set of forms for easy reference. An employer does not want to wade through a lengthy letter to find out if you match the set criteria. He or she has many applicants to choose from and, as such, your application will be dismissed if you do not conveniently conform.

Similarly, make sure you complete the application form fully. One of the initial criteria could be that you must have a clean driving licence. If the form was poorly laid out you might accidentally overlook this question and, therefore, be eliminated. Be careful!

With these points in mind you should then take the blank application form and photocopy it. Use the photocopy to practise on. Read it through first and jot down on a separate sheet of paper the points you want to put across in each section. Some are fairly simple. Some sections, however, can require detailed replies and you should, therefore, spend time deciding what you are going to say and how you are going to say it.

Always follow instructions. Read the form through carefully once again. Often it will ask you to complete it in black ink (which photocopies better than blue), in block capitals (which is easy to read) or in your handwriting (which some companies have analysed to read your character). If you did not follow such instructions, then your form could immediately be discarded. Some criteria for weeding out applicants are very petty.

Some employers would deny using such methods. It does, however, happen and, to be honest, why not? If you can't follow simple instructions now, what will you be like when you're working?

The form must be completed neatly. You will often be asked to write in block capitals anyway but even if you are not it can be sensible to do so especially if your handwriting is poor. Alternatively consider typing the application out if you or a friend can type.

Pay attention to spelling. Check with a dictionary if you're not sure how a word should be spelt. Pay attention to your grammar as well. Both are important especially if the job involves completing paperwork.

Always return the completed application form promptly by first class post or, alternatively, deliver it to the company yourself. *Always attach a supporting letter to the form.* As detailed in Chapter Four: Writing Letters, this will further highlight your strengths. Staple the letter to the form so that it will not become detached.

Make sure you have the correct name and address on the envelope. I know one recruiting officer who always rejects applicants who have not spelt his name correctly. Attention to detail is important.

COMPLETING AN APPLICATION FORM

Of course, all application forms vary in design, style and layout. A number of application forms from some of Britain's leading companies are given as examples at the end of this chapter. Read them through carefully. You will note that their contents tend to be similar. Most of them will want you to answer the same basic questions.

A typical application form – which will be examined in further detail – could read as follows:

APPLICATION FORM

SURNAME ....

FORENAME(S) ....

POSITION APPLIED FOR ....

CURRENT ADDRESS ....

TELEPHONE NUMBER..

DATE OF BIRTH ....

AGE ....

PLACE OF BIRTH ....

NATIONALITY..

MARITAL STATUS ....

MAIDEN NAME (IF APPLICABLE) ....

NUMBER OF CHILDREN ....

AGES..

EDUCATION

SCHOOL(S)	FROM	TO	EXAMINATIONS	DATES

COLLEGE(S)	FROM	TO	EXAMINATIONS	DATES

UNIVERSITY/ POLYTECHNIC	FROM	TO	EXAMINATIONS	DATES

Application forms

EMPLOYMENT

EMPLOYER	FROM	TO	POSITION AND DUTIES	SALARY	REASONS FOR LEAVING

HAVE YOU EVER HAD ANY SERIOUS ILLNESSES? ....
ARE YOU REGISTERED AS PHYSICALLY DISABLED? ....
WHAT IS YOUR HEIGHT? ....
WHAT IS YOUR WEIGHT? ....
DO YOU HAVE A CURRENT DRIVING LICENCE? ....
DO YOU HAVE ANY ENDORSEMENTS? ....
HOW DID YOU FIND OUT ABOUT THIS VACANCY? ....
WHAT WOULD BE YOUR REQUIRED SALARY? ....
ARE THERE ANY GEOGRAPHICAL LOCATIONS YOU
WOULD NOT BE PREPARED TO MOVE TO? ....
HOW SOON WOULD YOU BE AVAILABLE TO START WORK?

ADDITIONAL INFORMATION
(IS THERE ANY ADDITIONAL INFORMATION YOU
WOULD LIKE TO ADD TO SUPPORT YOUR
APPLICATION? WHY HAVE YOU APPLIED FOR THIS
JOB? WHAT OTHER QUALITIES OR EXPERIENCE DO
YOU HAVE WHICH ARE RELEVANT TO THIS
APPLICATION?)

REFERENCES
WE REQUIRE TWO REFERENCES TO SUPPORT YOUR
APPLICATION.

NAME ....   NAME ....
ADDRESS ....   ADDRESS ....
POSITION ....   POSITION.............................

I DECLARE THAT ALL STATEMENTS ARE TRUE. I
ACCEPT THAT ANY FALSE STATEMENTS WILL
RENDER ME LIABLE TO INSTANT DISMISSAL IF I AM
APPOINTED TO THIS POST.

SIGNATURE ....   DATE ....

Looking at the example of a typical application form you might complete it as follows. First, fill in your SURNAME and FORE-NAMES. Do remember to put them in the right boxes. Many people muddle them up, which can cause confusion if you had a name such as 'Michael James' or an unusual foreign one. It also looks sloppy and careless. Can't you read?

Complete the POSITION APPLIED FOR by using the job title indicated in the advertisement or job description. Also note down any reference number again. If you don't, your application may find its way onto the wrong pile.

Your CURRENT ADDRESS and TELEPHONE NUMBER are easy to complete. As with all sections do remember to make the address easy to read. Add the dialling code to the telephone number if appropriate. The employer may want to telephone you (see Chapter Five: Using the Telephone).

Make sure you can be reached on the phone number during the day or, alternatively, that there is someone available to take a message. There is nothing more annoying for an employer than to keep ringing an applicant without success. Your application form will probably end up in the waste paper basket.

Often a job advertisement will stipulate a minimum and maximum age for applicants and the employer will automatically turn to DATE OF BIRTH and AGE to quickly weed out unsuitable applicants. If you are above or below the age limits but feel strongly you could do the job well, you should complete these two sections but add an asterisk indicating that you will comment on this in your supporting letter (see Chapter Four: Writing Letters). If you leave DATE OF BIRTH or AGE blank or complete them without comment your application will be rejected. Add ★ and state:

'Please refer to attached letter/ADDITIONAL INFORMATION.

You could then comment along the lines of:

'I am above/ below the required age for this job. I do, however, believe I should be considered because. . . .' Then add your reasons. (Refer to Michael James' application form at the end of the chapter.)

PLACE OF BIRTH and NATIONALITY do not appear on all application forms but are, of course, easy to complete if they do. These sections, along with MARITAL STATUS, NUMBER OF CHILDREN and AGES are occasionally left blank by some applicants and a few have even been known to add comments such as 'This is of no relevance' or 'This is a personal matter'. It is true that discrimination against, for example, married women with young children does still exist in some organisations. It is unfair. Fortunately most employers are nowadays very aware of their responsibilities in this area and many actively adopt an anti-discrimination policy which is admirable. Whatever your personal reaction is to such questions, it is important that you answer every section on an application form. If you had young children you would, of course, have made arrangements for them to be looked after and you could therefore add a comment on this in your supporting letter or under ADDITIONAL INFORMATION if you wished.

(There are a number of books and pamphlets which you might care to read if the area of discrimination is of concern to you. These are listed in the bibliography at the back of this book.)

EDUCATION and EMPLOYMENT are dealt with in some detail in Chapter Three: 'Curricula Vitae', and to avoid repetition are not dealt with here. Read the appropriate sections now from page 77 onwards. Apply the information given to your own circumstances.

'HAVE YOU EVER HAD ANY SERIOUS ILLNESSES?', 'ARE YOU REGISTERED AS PHYSICALLY DISABLED?', 'WHAT IS YOUR HEIGHT?' and 'WHAT IS YOUR WEIGHT?' are included to discover how healthy you are. They are, of course, especially relevant if you are applying for a 'physical' job. Answer such questions honestly. If they are included it will indicate that the employer attaches considerable importance to your health and, with the last two, your appearance.

If you have had a serious illness you could obtain and attach a doctor's note to indicate you have fully recovered or, alternatively, that it will not affect you doing the job satisfactorily.

Similarly, if you are disabled you could explain your disability and stress that it would not affect your ability to do the job. As with all statements you make you should substantiate them. For example:

This will not, of course, affect my work at all. As you will note from 'Employment' I have had a similar job with the same duties and responsibilities for the past two years. I have given my manager, Mr Ovett, as a referee and he will confirm my suitability for this post.

You should, of course, never apologise for a disability but you should nevertheless explain that it will not affect your work.

If you are excessively overweight for your height, you could find you will be rejected especially if the work is strenuous or the company wishes (rightly or wrongly) to project a certain image. As such, this may not be the job for you. State your height and weight and if you feel it could have a negative effect on your application you could comment, for example:

I am a little overweight although I am dieting at present. (Substantiate this by then adding – I have lost a stone in the last eight weeks.)

If you are excessively overweight then, unless you had a genuine medical problem (which you could state), it would indicate you have little self control or interest in your appearance and your appearance is important in the job hunting process (see Chapter Seven: 'The Interview').

The questions DO YOU HAVE A CURRENT DRIVING LICENCE? and DO YOU HAVE ANY ENDORSEMENTS? may be included and are, of course, especially relevant if you are applying for a job which does, or could, involve driving. In such a situation you would obviously need a driving licence. More importantly, it should be clean. An employer will not want to employ someone who has a record of speeding or drink driving. What would he do if he employed you as a travelling salesman and you were stopped for speeding and banned? Clearly, he will be reluctant to take that risk.

Sometimes these questions may be asked even if the job does not involve driving. This may be because the company uses the same form for all types of vacancies or it may be that the job could lead to a promotion where driving would be involved. If you do not have a driving licence you would, of course, state

'No' but do not leave it at that. You may miss out on a good job opportunity. State, for example:

> No. I am, however, learning to drive as I think this would be an asset. You may, for example, wish me to transfer to your other outlets and with a car it would be easier for me to take advantage of such an opportunity.

(At this point remember not to highlight your weaknesses. You may have failed your driving test six times or knocked a post-man off his bike last time round. This is not the time or place to mention it.)

HOW DID YOU FIND OUT ABOUT THIS VACANCY? can also appear. This question is often included for the company's advantage to see how successful their advertising was and how many appli-cants actually saw or heard each advertisement. You can, how-ever, turn the answer to your advantage to show how thorough you are. Instead of simply jotting down 'I saw a newspaper advert' or 'a friend told me about it', try to add that little extra. For example:

> I check all the newspapers in the library each day and saw your advertisement in the 'Daily Echo' this morning.

Or (and this is better);

> I telephone the jobs section of the daily papers every day and they told me your advertisement was appearing in tomorrow's edition.

If you were really smart, you'd also ask the advertisement department of the company where they had advertised the job before you completed the form and could then state:

> I saw your advertisement for the vacancy in the 'Daily Echo', 'Daily Mercury' and 'Daily Times'. I also saw it in 'Catering Monthly' and 'The Bakers Bulletin'.

Most applicants would have simply scribbled down 'The Echo' or 'Mercury' or 'Daily Times' and thought nothing of it. You have scored a valuable point by showing how thorough and keen you are.

WHAT WOULD BE YOUR REQUIRED SALARY? can be a difficult question to answer. It is often used by an employer to weed out unsuitable applicants quickly. At this stage (when you are simply trying to obtain an interview) you must be tactful. You must be careful not to be eliminated by overpricing or underselling yourself. The employer will normally have a salary range in mind and if you quote a figure above that you will fail. Similarly if you quote too low a figure because you really want the job you could also fail because the employer will think that if you work for such a low salary you probably aren't very good at the job. So be careful.

You will normally see phrases in job advertisements such as 'Up to £17,000 per annum according to experience', 'salary open to negotiation' or 'salary to be discussed'. You could therefore state:

I would prefer to discuss this at the interview, please.

Or, if you prefer:

I would be looking for a salary in line with my experience and progress to date.

Or, (and this is the best):

At this stage in my career, the challenge your job offers is more important to me. I would like to negotiate an appropriate salary at a later date.

Whatever you put, the important point is that you do not knock yourself out by stating a fixed salary. Never, at this stage, quote a figure. Wait until the end of the interview when you know they're interested in you. You're then in a stronger bargaining position.

ARE THERE ANY GEOGRAPHICAL LOCATIONS YOU WOULD NOT BE PREPARED TO MOVE TO?' requires the obvious answer: 'No'. Clearly, if you stated you would not move, for example, 'down south' before you'd even been offered the job then, in all probability, you would not progress to the interview stage. You should therefore say something along the lines of

> No. I would be pleased (show some enthusiasm) to transfer to any of your outlets.

However, at the same time you don't want to indicate you're so desperate for work that you'd do anything anywhere so you should add a comment such as:

> No. I would be pleased to transfer to any of your outlets in the right circumstances.

This would indicate that you would be prepared to move if, for example, you were promoted or, perhaps, the company assisted with moving and re-location expenses.

HOW SOON WOULD YOU BE AVAILABLE TO START WORK? is normally included somewhere on the application form and the answer will, of course, depend on your current circumstances. If you are looking for your first job or are currently unemployed you could state:

> I am able to start work as soon as you wish.

or

> I can start work on the Monday following a satisfactory interview.

If you are currently employed and therefore have to hand in your notice you could say:

> I would be available to start work as from Monday 14th August.

or

> 'I have to give my current employers one week's notice. If possible I would like to give two weeks' notice as it would be of benefit to them. (You show you retain some loyalty and are keen to help them which is a sign of a good employee.) Perhaps we can discuss

this at the interview.' (It does no harm to mention the interview every so often to nudge them in the right direction).

ADDITIONAL INFORMATION is probably the most important section on the application form. Your chances of progressing to an interview will often depend on your response to it. Many applicants, nearing the end of an often lengthy form, will leave it blank because they can't think of anything to add. Those applicants are likely to fail.

The successful applicant will complete this section fully and, if necessary, add an additional page to the application form to complete his or her comments.

Firstly, read the section again. Most forms will add a question or two under the heading of ADDITIONAL INFORMATION. Read them and answer them. Take a separate sheet of paper, jot down the questions asked and the points you want to raise in response to each.

Following this you should read the entire application form again and compare it with other application forms you have seen. Are there any areas you have not been asked to comment on? Jot these areas down on that separate sheet of paper and again add any comments you want to make.

Looking, therefore, at the example given of a 'typical' application form you would jot down notes under the headings:

- I have applied for this job because   . . . . ?
                                        . . . . ?
                                        . . . . ?

- Other experience relevant to this application includes   . . . . ?
                                                           . . . . ?
                                                           . . . . ?

- My qualities include   . . . . ?
                         . . . . ?
                         . . . . ?

- My leisure interests include   – hobbies?
                                 – sports?
                                 – societies/clubs?
                                 – ?
                                 – ?

Clearly, the first three sub-sections relate to the questions asked and the fourth sub-section is an area which was not previously raised on the application form. Compile your own comments under each of these and then refer to Michael James' application form at the end of this chapter.

Some application forms, instead of having a section entitled ADDITIONAL INFORMATION, may have a page which simply asks you to comment on your experience and interests and to outline your career plans. In many ways this is a cross between ADDITIONAL INFORMATION and LETTERS OF APPLICATION which are discussed in Chapter Four: Writing Letters. Read both sections and then refer to Michael James' application form at the end of this chapter.

Often, you will be asked to complete this section in your own handwriting. As previously indicated, this may then be analysed. Graphology (the science of reading your character through your handwriting) often plays a serious role in recruitment procedures nowadays and the successful job hunter will be aware of it. There are a number of books available which look at this subject in more detail. These are listed in the bibliography at the back of the book. Read them.

You will, of course, need to provide REFERENCES. As indicated, you will usually have to give the names, addresses and positions of two people, or 'referees', who will give you a reference. The employer will normally ask them a number of questions. Examples of such letters from employers to referees are given on pages 67 and 71.

Basically, an employer wants to know that you are honest, reliable and hardworking. He will, therefore, want references from people who know you well. He will also want to be sure that they themselves are honest and trustworthy and, as such, will want referees who are of some standing in the community.

He will expect a reference from your current (or last) employer or a school (or college) reference from your tutor, head of year or headteacher. He would also accept a personal reference if that referee has known you for several years and, as indicated, was of some standing. Many texts indicate that a reference should be from someone such as a bank manager, solicitor or accountant and, of course, these would be ideal, but many other people would be suitable too. Do you, for example know a small businessman, a librarian, a civil servant or anyone else who has a respectable or responsible job? Be sensible though. One applicant gave me a bank clerk as a personal referee and she appeared ideal. I subsequently discovered however that she was his re-married mother!

When choosing your referees (and if you are a school or college leaver you would normally select a teacher and an employer if you had a part-time job) you should ask them first of all if they would act as referees for you. They are, after all, doing you a favour and if you look at the examples of letters sent by employers to referees you'll realise that a reply can take time to compile, write and send. Always be polite and courteous. Ask them first.

References will not normally be taken up until after the interview. When you know that your referees are about to be approached, you should again write or telephone them to let them know that a prospective employer will be writing. Tell them about the job and why you think you can do it well. It will encourage them to comment on your strengths in their replies.

You should write or ring your referees again after they have given you a reference just to thank them. It is polite and, after all, they may have helped you to obtain the job.

Incidentally, some job hunters collect lengthy pre-written references which they then attach to an application form, curriculum vitae or letter of application. Do not do this. They can become dated, may lose their appearance if they are sent back and forth to many employers and are often viewed with suspicion (do you think he's written these himself/told them what to write?) In addition such references may not be directly relevant to this particular job and may not answer all the questions the employer would ask. Wait until you're asked for references and, after giving names and addresses, let the employer contact them.

Finally, you will need to sign and date the application form and state that all the information is correct and that false statements could lead to your instant dismissal. Clearly it is therefore important that you do not lie as many applicants do, for example, when detailing qualifications or experience. The truth has a nasty habit of coming out and, as a result, you could lose your job. What would you then do when you applied for the next job? How would you explain why you had left? Who would you give as a referee? Remember, cheats never prosper. Stick to the truth.

To further assist you in completing an application form, here is a final example.

Michael James is applying for the job of trainee manager at a bakery. He has obtained a job description which he reads through carefully before completing the form. (No other documents were available from the company.) This particular application form asks him to complete it in block capitals. It also asks him to complete the ADDITIONAL INFORMATION section in his normal handwriting. (We have, however, printed this section to make it clearer.) His completed application form is on pages 40–44.

Michael should, of course, send his application form with a supporting letter. This should further highlight his strengths. Read 'Supporting Letters' in Chapter Four and then, looking at the comments Michael made in his ADDITIONAL INFORMATION, consider what you think should be written in his letter. You may find it helpful.

On the following pages you will find examples of 'real' application forms as used by ICI PLC and Wimpy International.

APPLICATION FORM

SURNAME ...JAMES...............................

FORENAME(S) ...MICHAEL...................

POSITION APPLIED FOR ...TRAINEE MANAGER (TM 10)...

CURRENT ADDRESS ...13 SHOTLEY ROAD THRETFORD, SURREY KP17 8WO

TELEPHONE NUMBER ...(0446) 9299...

DATE OF BIRTH ...5 SEPTEMBER 1970...

AGE ...19... (PLEASE REFER TO 'ADDITIONAL INFORMATION')

PLACE OF BIRTH ...THRETFORD, SURREY...

NATIONALITY ...BRITISH...

MARITAL STATUS ...SINGLE...

MAIDEN NAME (IF APPLICABLE) ...N/A...

NUMBER OF CHILDREN ...NONE...

AGES ...N/A...

EDUCATION

SCHOOL(S)	FROM	TO	EXAMINATIONS	DATES
THRETFORD SECONDARY	SEPTEMBER 1982	JUNE 1989	GCSE ENGLISH LITERATURE (C)	JUNE 1988
17 ABBEY ROAD			GCSE ENGLISH LANGUAGE (C)	JUNE 1988
THRETFORD, SURREY			GCSE HISTORY (B)	JUNE 1988
			GCSE GEOGRAPHY (B)	JUNE 1988
			GCSE MATHS (A)	JUNE 1988
			GCSE FRENCH (A)	JUNE 1988
			A LEVEL FRENCH (B)	JUNE 1990
			A LEVEL BUSINESS STUDIES (B)	JUNE 1990
			A LEVEL MATHS (B)	JUNE 1990

COLLEGE(S)	FROM	TO	EXAMINATIONS	DATES

←——————————— N/A ———————————→

UNIVERSITY/ POLYTECHNIC	FROM	TO	EXAMINATIONS	DATES

←——————————— N/A ———————————→

EMPLOYMENT

EMPLOYER	FROM	TO	POSITION AND DUTIES	SALARY	REASONS FOR LEAVING
PLATEKS BAKERY 4 THE HIGH STREET THRETFORD, SURREY	JULY 1987	—	I AM EMPLOYED AS A BAKER AND SHOP ASSISTANT	—	—

HAVE YOU EVER HAD ANY SERIOUS ILLNESSES? ....NO.......

ARE YOU REGISTERED AS PHYSICALLY DISABLED? ..NO.......

WHAT IS YOUR HEIGHT? ..6FT 2INS...

WHAT IS YOUR WEIGHT? ..12 ST 7.....

DO YOU HAVE A CURRENT DRIVING LICENCE? .YES...

DO YOU HAVE ANY ENDORSEMENTS? ..NO...

HOW DID YOU FIND OUT ABOUT THIS VACANCY? I HAVE BEEN WRITING REGULARLY TO YOUR PERSONNEL DEPARTMENT FOR THE LAST YEAR TO ENQUIRE ABOUT VACANCIES. MY LATEST LETTER ARRIVED ON THE DAY YOU CREATED THIS VACANCY.

WHAT WOULD BE YOUR REQUIRED SALARY? I UNDERSTAND THE SALARY IS NEGOTIABLE, COULD WE DISCUSS THIS FURTHER AT AN INTERVIEW?

ARE THERE ANY GEOGRAPHICAL LOCATIONS YOU WOULD NOT BE PREPARED TO MOVE TO? NO. I WOULD BE PLEASED TO RE-LOCATE IF IT WOULD BE A GOOD CAREER MOVE. I UNDERSTAND YOU ARE PLANNING TO OPEN A NEW OUTLET IN WOKING. I WOULD, FOR EXAMPLE, BE HAPPY TO MOVE THERE IF IT WAS A STEP IN THE RIGHT DIRECTION.

HOW SOON WOULD YOU BE AVAILABLE TO START WORK?   MONDAY 18 SEPTEMBER

ADDITIONAL INFORMATION

(IS THERE ANY ADDITIONAL INFORMATION YOU WOULD LIKE TO ADD TO SUPPORT
YOUR APPLICATION? WHY HAVE YOU APPLIED FOR THIS JOB? WHAT OTHER
QUALITIES OR EXPERIENCE DO YOU HAVE WHICH ARE RELEVANT TO THIS
APPLICATION?)

PLEASE REFER TO THE ADDITIONAL SHEET ATTACHED
TO THIS APPLICATION FORM.

REFERENCES

WE REQUIRE TWO REFERENCES TO SUPPORT YOUR APPLICATION.

NAME ...MR. W. COOPER.   NAME .MR. F. PLATEK......

ADDRESS THRETFORD. SECONDARY   ADDRESS PLATEK'S. BAKERY. LTD
                   SCHOOL
         17. ABBEY. ROAD.   4. THE. HIGH. STREET
         THRETFORD, SURREY   THRETFORD, SURREY

POSITION HEADMASTER...   POSITION PROPRIETOR........

I DECLARE THAT ALL STATEMENTS ARE TRUE. I ACCEPT THAT ANY FALSE
STATEMENTS WILL RENDER ME LIABLE TO INSTANT DISMISSAL IF I AM
APPOINTED TO THIS POST.

SIGNATURE Michael James   DATE 6 SEPTEMBER 1989

42

ADDITIONAL INFORMATION

I have applied for the post of trainee manager for a
number of reasons.   I have always enjoyed cooking and,
in particular, baking.   It is my hobby.   I also hope
to be fortunate enough to make it part of my career.
In addition, I would like a career which will stimulate
and challenge me and I believe a career in management
would do this.   I also want to be successful and fulfil
my potential.   I believe, therefore, that this job and,
more importantly, your company offer me the chance to
achieve all my hopes and ambitions.

I believe I can offer you considerable experience.
Since July, 1987 I have worked at 'Plateks Bakery'.
This has been a full time position during school holidays.
During term time I worked in the bakery before school and
at weekends.   Mr Platek, the proprietor, has taught me a
great deal about the trade.   I have also learned about
the business side of the bakery.   I have dealt with
suppliers and, of course, customers.   I even ran the
bakery for two weeks in the summer when Mr and Mrs Platek
went away on holiday.

I have no specific qualifications for the bakery trade
although many may consider I am fully qualified in terms
of my experience.   Rather than study a course at catering
college I chose to study 'A' levels which I thought would
be of benefit for a career in management.   As you will
see, I studied Business Studies and Maths which should be
helpful.   I also studied French in case you plan to expand
even further!   I have also studied Book-keeping at evening

43

school which I thought may help me too.

In my spare time I enjoy baking cakes.   I run this as
a little business and specialise in baking birthday cakes
for children.   I enclose photographs of some of the more
unusual cakes I have made!

Finally, I know I am below the minimum age.   I believe,
however, that I fulfil all your other requirements well
and, given the opportunity of an interview, I hope I could
prove that, in this instance, my age would not be a
problem.

Imperial Chemical Industries PLC

Personal Particulars

Private & Confidential

Please use black ink or black ball point

Forenames in full	Surname (in block letters)
Maiden name if married woman	Mr. Mrs. Miss/Ms

Permanent address	Temporary address (if any), with dates
Telephone No. Post Code	Telephone No. Post Code

Nationality	Place of Birth	Date of Birth			Marital status	If registered under Disabled Persons (Employment) Act, state
		Day	Month	Year		Registration No.
Do you need a work permit to take up employment in the UK?						Expiry Date of Certificate

Education

Secondary Schools (names & towns) and College of Further Education (state whether part-time/full-time)	From Yr/Month	To Yr/Month	Details of Courses taken	
			Subjects/courses studied, and level	Exam results and year obtained

University/Polytechnic (state college where applicable)	From Yr/Month	To Yr/Month	Degree(s) & type	Class obtained	Principal subject(s)	Subsidiary subject(s)
					Subject of Post-Graduate Research (if any)	

Details of scholarships, studentships or Public Prizes won at School and/or University Polytechnic	
Professional or other qualifications, including membership of Professional and/or Scientific Societies (including date admitted where relevant)	
Details of other specialised training, knowledge or experience, eg. apprenticeships, shorthand and typing (speeds obtained), current driving licence	
Knowledge of foreign language(s) (indicate proficiency, spoken and written).	
Other interests (societies, hobbies, sports, etc). Indicate any posts of responsibility, and relevant dates.	

SP 1A

45

Previous employment in ICI (if any)

Have you ever been in the employment of ICI or
any of its subsidiary or associated companies?
If so, give Division, location, job held and dates

Reason for leaving

Introduction

Introduction (if any, eg. employment bureau,
newspaper advert, careers directory, friend,
relative etc) (please be specific)

Further personal details

We shall need this personal information if you join the Company (eg. for Pension Funds)
but if you prefer it may be given when you accept a job offer.

Date of marriage (if applicable)			Date of birth of wife/husband (if applicable)			Forenames of wife/husband	Date of birth of children (if any)			
Day	Month	Year	Day	Month	Year		Day	Month	Year	M or F

Are you currently a member of a pension/superannuation scheme? Yes/No

If yes, (a) to which pension or superannuation scheme do you belong?
(b) do you wish to consider a transfer of rights?

Supplementary information you may wish to include	This information is needed to assist ICI with the practice of its Equal Opportunities Policies in order to prevent discrimination from taking place.					
	I would describe my ethnic origins as (please circle one of the following):–					
	African	Asian	Caribbean	UK/Irish	Other European	Other (please specify)
	1	2	3	4	5	6

References

Give two references. Where appropriate, one of
these should be from your present or latest
employer, or from your head teacher/tutor.

**Please mark X against any that you do not
want taken up at this stage.**

Note:
a) References will not be taken up before you
are called for interview.
b) Original testimonials must not be forwarded.

1 Name ....

Address ....

....

Telephone No. ....

2 Name ....

Address ....

....

Telephone No. ....

This form should be sent to

Signature ....

Date ....

Birmingham Press Limited

Employment sought in ICI

Type of work sought	Expected Salary	How soon could you enter employment, if appointed	Geographical preference (if any)
	£ pa		

Employment history

If you are a student or have graduated or left school/college recently

Give details of:

(a) Employment/professional experience which formed part of a Sandwich Course; with dates and name of employer

(b) Vacation or temporary employment

Full-time employment – present or latest employment

Name and Address of Employer	Date started			
		Basic salary	£	pa
		Bonus	£	
	Date left (if applicable)	Other remuneration	£	pa
		Other benefits (eg, car allowance)		
Employer's business				

Brief description of work and experience gained (indicating responsibilities)

Reason for leaving

Employment previous to above (latest employment first)

Name and Address of Employer	Date started	Date left	Reason for leaving
	Salary at leaving		
	Basic £ pa		
Employer's business	Total £ pa		

Brief description of work and experience gained (indicating responsibilities)

Name and Address of Employer	Date started	Date left	Reason for leaving
	Salary at leaving		
	Basic £ pa		
Employer's business	Total £ pa		

Brief description of work and experience gained (indicating responsibilities)

Service in the Forces (including branch of service, dates and highest rank held). If you have been rejected or discharged on medical grounds, what was your grading?

(Please attach separate sheet for further work experience (if applicable)

Description of career

In your own handwriting, outline your career expectations and aspirations, both in the short and longer term. Expand on any work experience or interests which you feel are relevant to your application.

WIMPY INTERNATIONAL

is a member of the United Biscuits Group

APPLICATION   FOR   APPOINTMENT

FROM

FULL NAME _____

POSITION APPLIED FOR _____

PREFERRED AREA FOR EMPLOYMENT IN U.K. _____

COMPLETED APPLICATION FORM SHOULD BE SENT TO:–

PERSONNEL MANAGER
WIMPY INTERNATIONAL
10 Windmill Road
London, W4 1SD

OTHER RELEVANT
INFORMATION — Please add any other information which you feel may be relevant, e.g. published work, research work, any particular interests, reason for applying.

Membership of any Professional Association, Institute or Society

Do you hold a current Driving Licence? YES/NO. Number of endorsements ....

HEALTH (Employment is subject to a satisfactory medical examination)

Nature and dates of any serious illness/accident/operation	Do you have any physical disability?	Are you a registered disabled person? If yes, please give certificate no.
	If so, please state nature of disability	HEIGHT: WEIGHT:

Have you ever been the subject of any Police enquiries regarding your honesty?

I declare that the above information is accurate and complete. I understand that any false statement or witholding of information may make me liable to disqualification, or if appointed, to dismissal.

Signed: _____   *Date:* _____

FOR OFFICE USE ONLY

INTERVIEWER'S NOTES:

107 PS

50

Surname _____ First names _____

Mr/Mrs/Miss/Ms   Single ☐   Married ☐   Divorced ☐   Separated ☐   Widow(er) ☐

Date of Birth _____ Age _____ Place of Birth _____

Present Nationality _____ No. of Children _____

Their ages _____

Permanent Address	Name & Address of person to contact in case of emergency

Tel. No. _____   Tel. No. _____

How did you find out about this vacancy? _____

If you saw an advertisement, where was it? _____

If not, give source _____

When could you take up a new appointment?   Salary required ....

EDUCATION AND TRAINING — please detail all qualifications gained

Secondary Schools	Dates From	To	Examination Results	Dates Obtained
Further Education to include any training courses			Degrees or Diplomas obtained	

LANGUAGES — indicate proficiency as fluent, working knowledge or slight knowledge

LANGUAGE	SPOKEN	WRITTEN	READING

PREVIOUS EMPLOYMENT — Please begin with present or last Employer

Name and address of employer	Dates From To	Position held and duties performed	Gross Salary	Reason for leaving

PRESENT APPOINTMENT — Please expand the brief details given earlier indicating the range of your responsibilities

REFERENCES — please give previous employers wherever possible.

Name
Address

Name
Address

Position

Position

Application Form for Appointment

Please write clearly and tick boxes ✓

1 I apply for appointment as Police Constable ☐   Police Cadet ☐

2 Surname   Initials

3 It is in your own interest to complete this application form as accurately as possible. The answers you give will help us decide whether you have the basic potential for appointment. Please remember to:

- use BLACK ink;
- answer ALL questions—writing 'NIL' where appropriate;
- use BLOCK LETTERS on pages 1 – 3 and 5 – 10;
- use normal handwriting on page 4;
- use the continuation sheet at page 6 if you need more space for any answer;
- sign the declarations on pages 9 and 11.

4 Every effort will be made to process your application as quickly as possible. However, the post of Constable carries considerable responsibility and full, careful enquiries have to be made about all candidates. These may take some time to complete. If you want to ask about the progress of your application please contact the Selection Centre.

5 **Applicants for Police Constable**

Please send your completed form to:
   The Recruiting Officer
   Metropolitan Police Selection Centre
   FREEPOST
   London W2 1BR

Applicants for Police Cadet

Please send your completed form to:
   The Recruiting Officer
   Metropolitan Police Selection Centre
   FREEPOST
   Aerodrome Road
   London NW9 7YP

For official use only

T/U	AE	PIR	HM	COLL UNIV	OPT	HW	S	Q	Date Stamp

Form 6068/6069

Equal Opportunity Statement

The Metropolitan Police is committed to being an equal opportunity employer and is determined to ensure that no job applicant or employee who satisfies the requirements set out in footnote § on page 1 overleaf:

- receives less favourable treatment on the grounds of sex or marital status, colour, race, nationality, ethnic or national origins; or
- is disadvantaged by conditions or requirements which cannot be shown to be justified.

We also seek to ensure that employees are not victimised or sexually harassed. In accordance with the Codes of Practice issued by the Commission for Racial Equality and the Equal Opportunities Commission the Metropolitan Police records the ethnic origin and sex of people who apply for appointment.

To implement and monitor the effectiveness of its equal opportunity policy the Metropolitan Police would be grateful if you would complete the table below.

If you have any queries about this form please contact the Metropolitan Police Careers Advice Office, telephone number 01-725 4492, or visit one of our careers advisers at the Careers Office, New Scotland Yard, Victoria Street, London SW1H 0BG

Thank you for your co-operation

THE INFORMATION YOU GIVE HERE WILL NOT AFFECT YOUR APPLICATION

Please tick the appropriate boxes

I am applying to become a Cadet ☐	Constable ☐
I am Female ☐	Male ☐
Married ☐	Single ☐
Separated ☐ Divorced ☐	Widowed ☐

I would describe my ethnic origin as: —

BLACK	WHITE
Afro-Caribbean ☐	European (including U.K.) ☐
African ☐	
Asian ☐	
Other (please specify) ☐	Other (please specify) ☐

_____   _____

54

1. Details of Candidate

Surname (now)	Previous Surname
Full forename(s)	
Address	
	Postcode
Telephone No. Home	Work
Age* years months	Date of Birth
Nationality §	

*Although the normal upper age limit for joining the police is 30 we will consider applicants up to the age of 40.

§To be eligible for appointment you must be:

- (a) a British citizen or a citizen of the Irish Republic; or
- (b) a Commonwealth citizen (other than a British citizen) in which case you must satisfy one of the following conditions: —
  - (i) at least one of your parents must be, or have been at death, a Commonwealth citizen; or
  - (ii) you must have resided in a country or territory within the Commonwealth or have been employed elsewhere in the service of the Crown, or partly have so resided and partly been so employed for at least 5 out of the last 8 years.

In addition you must have the right to live permanently in the United Kingdom.

2. Education

The purpose of these questions is to see whether you will be required to sit the standard entrance test. You will be required to produce education certificates if invited for interview. If you are still in or have recently left full-time education, we will ask for a reference from the place concerned.

(a) Please enter details of your education from the age of 11

Name and address of school/college	Attendance		
	From	To	Full or part time

55

(b) Please enter details of examinations you have passed or are due to take

Examination (CSE, GCE, GCSE, Degree etc.)	Date passed	Grade obtained	Date due to be taken

3. Particulars of any application to or service in a Police Force

If you have previously applied to join another Force, considerable time could be saved if we can obtain from them details of any enquiries they have already made.

(a) Please give details of any application (including current applications) for appointment e.g., Cadet, Constable, Civil Staff, Special Constabulary. Details of previous applications to this Force should also be included.

Date	Name of Force	Type of Appointment	Result

(b) Please give details of service in any police force

Name of Force	Capacity in which employed	Dates of Service		Reason for leaving (if applicable)
		From	To	

4. Details of any service in H.M. Forces

Served with
H.M. Armed Forces
(tick appropriate box)

Royal Navy ☐   Royal Marines ☐

Army ☐   Royal Air Force ☐

Service No.	Rank or Rating
Corps or Regiment (Army)	Branch (R.N. & R.A.F.)
Service From To	Expected Date of Discharge
Reason for Discharge	
Service Character Assessment	

5. Employment History

(a) Please provide, in sequence, details of any full, part-time or casual employment you have had

Name, address and nature of business of employer	Position held and main duties	Dates		Reason for leaving
		Started	Left	

(b) Present Employer*

Name, address and nature of business of employer	Position held and main duties	Date started	Reason for wanting to leave

*We will not make any enquiries of your present employer unless we recommend you for appointment.

6. Achievements

What do you consider to be your main achievements in your education and career, including any awards or prizes you have won or positions of responsibility you have held?

7. Interests

Please describe your leisure interests, including any voluntary/community work.

8. Why do you wish to join the Metropolitan Police?

9. Convictions/Cautions

(a) Please enter below details of convictions for any offence (including traffic convictions and appearances before a Court Martial) or formal cautions by police for any offence (including cautions as a juvenile) or any bind-overs imposed by any Court. You must include spent convictions under the Rehabilitation of Offenders Act 1974 (by virtue of the provisions of the Rehabilitation of Offenders Act 1974 (Exceptions) Order 1975).

If you have been convicted or cautioned you may still be eligible for appointment depending on the nature and circumstances of the offence. However, failure to disclose details could count against you.

Date	Court/Police Station which dealt with the matter	Offence(s)	Result

(b) Please give details of any charge or summons at present outstanding against you

Date of alleged offence	Nature of alleged offence	Court/Police Station dealing with the matter

10. Have you ever been tattooed?

If YES, give the details required.

YES or NO	Describe all the tattoos here. Enclose colour photographs of all of them.

	CONTINUATION SHEET
Question	**Details**

MEDICAL HISTORY

The questions in this section enable the Chief Medical Officer to decide if you are medically suitable for consideration or if he requires additional medical information before reaching a decision.

The information you give here will be treated in strict confidence.

Surname.. Forenames ....

Age.............................. Male or Female *..

Height (in bare feet)................ft. .... ins.   OR   ....cms

Weight (in ordinary clothing)................ st.   ....lbs.   OR   .... kgs

*You are asked to state whether you are male or female because the Police Regulations impose different height requirements for men and women. These height requirements are similar to the average heights for men and women in this country.

Please answer **ALL** the following questions. If you need more space for any answer, please continue on the medical history continuation sheet at page 10.

1. Have you ever suffered from any of the following?
Please state YES or NO and if YES give the details required.

	YES or NO	Nature of illness and treatment	Dates	
			From	To
Fever				
Enlargement of glands				
Spitting blood				
Asthma				
Bronchitis				
Pleurisy				
Inflammation of the lungs or tuberculosis				
Heart disease				
Fainting attacks				
Appendicitis				
Other abdominal disorders				
Dyspepsia				
Diarrhoea				
Discharge from the ear				
Hearing defect				
Venereal disease				
Skin disorder				
Rheumatism				
Arthritis				
Recurring headaches				
Migraine				
Any nervous disease				

61

Medical History — Continued

	YES or NO	Nature of illness and treatment	Dates From	To
Any mental, psychiatric or phobic illness				
Epileptic fit				
Convulsions				
Peptic, gastric or duodenal ulcer				
Injury to bones, tendons or joints				
Enuresis (bed wetting)				
Varicose veins				
Squint or other morbid condition of the eyes or eyelids				
Eyesight defect				
Any allergic disorders				
Any congenital or acquired malformation, defect or deformity				

2. Have any of your close relatives suffered from the following?

	YES or NO	Relationship
Tuberculosis		
Asthma		
Epileptic fit		
Nervous disease		
Mental, psychiatric or phobic illness		

3. Please answer the following

	YES or NO	Nature of illness and treatment	Dates From	To
Have you ever had a surgical operation?				
Have you ever been an in-patient in hospital?				
Have you been prescribed any medication/drugs by your doctor during the past 5 years? *				
Are you currently receiving any form of medical supervision or treatment? *				
Have you ever been tested for HIV antibodies (A.I.D.S.)?		If YES, what was the result?		

* Candidates need not declare medication or treatment prescribed solely for contraceptive purposes.

4. Have you ever been medically examined as follows?

	YES or NO	Result of Medical
For life insurance?		
By any government medical officer, civil or military?		

5. Do you wear the following?

	YES or NO	If YES, please enclose the information required
Vision aids (Spectacles or contact lenses)		Optician's certificate showing the acuity (keenness) of vision in each eye and both eyes together with and WITHOUT artificial aids (Snellens test)
Dentures		A brief note from your dental surgeon describing their extent, for the information of our consulting dental surgeon.

6. Please answer the following

	YES or NO	Daily consumption
Do you smoke?		
Do you drink alcohol?		

7. Is there any other matter concerning your health not covered by the above questions which the Chief Medical Officer should know about?

YES or NO	Details

I declare that the statements I have made on this form are true to the best of my knowledge and belief. I will fully reveal to the Chief Medical Officer everything I know about my health and fitness for the appointment for which I am a candidate.

Date [   ]   Signature of Applicant [   ]

Signature of parent or guardian
(if the applicant is under 18 years of age) [   ]

NOTE: PLEASE ALSO READ CAREFULLY AND SIGN THE DECLARATION ON PAGE 11

	MEDICAL HISTORY CONTINUATION SHEET
Question	**Details**

DECLARATION

I understand a member of a police force who has deliberately made any false statement or omitted information in connection with his or her appointment commits an offence under the Discipline Code set out in the Police (Discipline) Regulations and is liable to punishment accordingly. I declare that all the statements I have made in this application are true to the best of my knowledge and belief.

Date...

SIGNATURE OF APPLICANT

....

SIGNATURE OF PARENT OR GUARDIAN
(if the applicant is under 18 years of age and you
agree to this application)

Note: i) Information supplied on this form may be held on computer and candidates are advised that in processing this application background enquiries will be made which may include reference to personal data held on police computers.

ii) The Commissioner retains the right to reject any application without giving a reason.

The height/weight ratios normally applied to candidates for the Metropolitan Police are reproduced below.

If your weight in relation to your height is above or below the ideal weights shown in the chart, do not feel that you are ineligible to apply. We would be pleased to consider an application although our Chief Medical Officer and Director of Physical Training would need to assure themselves that you would be medically and physically fit to undertake police training and duties.

All candidates invited for interview will have to undergo physical fitness tests to prove stamina and body strength as part of the selection procedure. You will be sent full details of the tests if we proceed with your application.

MALE				FEMALE			
HEIGHT		ACCEPTABLE WEIGHT		HEIGHT		ACCEPTABLE WEIGHT	
CMS	FEET/INCHES	MINIMUM	MAXIMUM	CMS	FEET/INCHES	MINIMUM	MAXIMUM
200	6'7"			190			
199				189			
198	6'6"			188	6'2"		
197	.			187			
196		11 stone		186	6'1"		
195	6'5"	(70 Kg)		185			13 stone
194			15st 7lbs	184		9 stone	(82.5Kg)
193	6'4"		(98.5Kg)	183	6'0"	(57 Kg)	
192				182			
191				181			
190	6'3"	10st71bs		180	5'11"		
189		(66.5Kg)		179			
188	6'2"			178	5'10"		
187				177			
186	6'1"		15 stone	176			
185			95.3 Kg)	175	5'9"		12st 71b
184				174		8st 71bs	(79.5Kg)
183	6'0"			173	5'8"	(54 Kg)	
182				172			12 stone
181		10 stone		171			(76 Kg)
180	5'11"	(63.5Kg)	14st 71bs	170	5'7"		
179			(92 Kg)	169			
178	5'10"			168	5'6"	8 stone	11st 71b
177				167		(51 Kg)	(73 Kg)
176				166			
175	5'9"	9st 71bs	13st 71bs	165	5'5"		
174		(60.5Kg)	(85.6Kg)	164			
173	5'8"			163	5'4"	7st 71b	11 stone
172				162		(47.5Kg)	(70 Kg)

66

Imperial
Chemical
Industries
PLC

SLTR-1/DOC6
REFERENCE REQUEST BEFORE OFFER OF EMPLOYMENT

_____
_____
_____
_____

Your ref   Our ref   Tel ext   Date

_____   _____   _____   _____

Dear _____

Your name has been given to us as a referee by _____.

Before we make a formal offer of appointment it would be most
helpful if you could inform us, in confidence, whether you consider
he/she would be an honest and trustworthy member of our staff. It
would help us if you could, in addition, give us any information
about him/her character and general ability.

We shall be very grateful for any assistance that you may give us,
and enclose an envelope for your reply.

Yours sincerely

_____
Personnel Officer
Head Office Personnel Section

Imperial Chemical House
Millbank London SW1P 3JF

Telephone 01-834 4444
Telex 21324

Imperial
Chemical
Industries
PLC

SLTR-1/DOC7
REFERENCE REQUEST AFTER OFFER OF EMPLOYMENT

_____
_____
_____
_____
_____

Your ref	Our ref	Tel ext	Date
_____	_____	____	_____

Dear _____

Your name has been given to us as a referee by _____.

We have made a formal offer of appointment to the above and it would
be most helpful if you could inform us, in confidence, whether you
consider <u>he/she</u> would be an honest and trustworthy member of our
staff. It would help us if you could, in addition, give us any
information about <u>his/her</u> character and general ability.

We should be very grateful for any assistance that you may give us
and we enclose an envelope for your reply.

Yours sincerely

_____
Personnel Officer
Head Office Personnel Section

68

WIMPY INTERNATIONAL

10 Windmill Road Chiswick London W4 1SD   01 994 6454 Telex 935278 Fax No. 01 995 0563

OUR REF:LJW:CAE   1 November 1988

PRIVATE AND CONFIDENTIAL

Personnel Department
J Middleton Ltd
Power Road
Chiswick
London
W4

Dear Sir/Madam,

<u>MR MICHAEL JAMES</u>

The above mentioned person has applied to us for employment and to assist us to
assess his suitability, we would be grateful if you would be kind enough to
complete the questionnaire below. Naturally, any information you may give us
would be treated in the strictest confidence.

A pre-paid envelope is enclosed and we thank you in anticipation of your reply.

Yours faithfully

LINDA J WOODS
PERSONNEL MANAGER

1. Length of service - From .... To ....

2. Capacity in which employed ....

3. Reason for leaving ....

4. How would you rate applicant, eg, good, average, poor, with regard to:-

    (a) Ability .... (b) Time-keeping ....

    (c) Conduct .... (d) Health ....

5. Have you any reason to doubt his/her honesty ....

6. Would you re-employ ....

Signed ....   Date ....

Position ....

UB A Division of United Biscuits (UK) Ltd. Registered in Scotland, Number 31456 · Registered Office: 12 Hope Street, Edinburgh

METROPOLITAN POLICE OFFICE
CADET SELECTION CENTRE
HENDON CADET TRAINING SCHOOL
AERODROME ROAD, HENDON
LONDON, NW9 5JH
Telephone 01-200 2271

Your ref.:   Our ref.:

Re: _____

At school from: To:

Dear Head Teacher,

The above named person has applied to join the Metropolitan Police Cadet Corps and
states that he/she attended your school as shown above.

In order to assist in the consideration of this applicant, the Commissioner would be
glad of your comments on this person's school record and general character please.
A pro-forma appears on the reverse of this letter if you prefer to give your
observations under specified headings.

I am sure you will appreciate the need for the most thorough enquiries to be made
in respect of potential members of the police service, and I would therefore ask
that your comments be as objective and candid as possible.

All information supplied is treated in the strictest confidence.

An early reply would be greatly appreciated, and a pre-paid label is enclosed.

Yours faithfully,

for Recruiting Officer.

**METROPOLITAN POLICE OFFICE
CADET SELECTION CENTRE**
HENDON CADET TRAINING SCHOOL
AERODROME ROAD, HENDON
LONDON, NW9 5JH
Telephone 01—200 2272 Ext.

Your ref.:	Our ref.:

Dear

The above named person has made application for appointment as a Cadet with
this Force and has nominated you to act as a referee. In order to consider
this application further, it would be appreciated if you would kindly
complete the questionnaire overleaf and return it to this office using the
stamped addressed envelope enclosed.

I am sure you will appreciate the need for the most thorough enquiries to be
made in respect of potential members of the police service and would,
therefore, ask that your comments be as objective and candid as possible.

Your co-operation in this matter would be greatly appreciated and I can assure
you that your reply will be treated as strictly confidential.

Yours sincerely,

for Recruiting Officer

CHAPTER THREE

CURRICULA VITAE

THE CURRICULUM VITAE FRAMEWORK

PREPARATION

COMPILATION
- PERSONAL DETAILS
- EDUCATION
- EXPERIENCE
- LEISURE INTERESTS

CHAPTER THREE

CURRICULA VITAE

A curriculum vitae, or 'C.V', is simply a timetable of your life. It indicates your track record to date. Many organisations, as previously indicated, will ask applicants to send a C.V. with a supporting letter. If you are applying to an organisation 'on spec' you could also send a C.V. with a supporting letter (refer to Chapter Four: Writing Letters). A curriculum vitae is usually drawn up around the following framework:

CURRICULUM VITAE
PERSONAL DETAILS
NAME:
ADDRESS:
TELEPHONE NUMBER   (HOME):
                        (WORK):
AGE:
DATE OF BIRTH:
MARITAL STATUS:
DEPENDANTS: (AND AGES)

EDUCATION
SCHOOL(S):   (WITH DATES)
COLLEGE(S):   (WITH DATES)
UNIVERSITY: (WITH DATES)
QUALIFICATIONS: (SUBJECTS, GRADES,
                              DATES, EXAMINING
                              BODIES)

ACTIVITIES:
POSTS OF RESPONSIBILITY:

EXPERIENCE
NAME OF ORGANISATION(S), LOCATIONS(S), JOB
TITLE(S), DATES, DUTIES,
REASONS FOR LEAVING.
LEISURE INTERESTS
HOBBIES:
CLUBS/SOCIETIES:

PREPARATION

You must take time to prepare your curriculum vitae. It is, after all, an advertisement for you and is also your first point of contact with a prospective employer. Your success depends upon getting it right.

There are a number of points to consider before you compile your C.V. It should be no more than two to three sides of A4 paper in length. It must be typed and double-spaced on one side of the paper only. Use good quality paper. It should look professional. If you cannot type yourself or do not have access to a typewriter, then you must invest in the services of a typing agency. Look on noticeboards around college or in newsagents' windows. Have perhaps fifty C.V's typed up (depending, of course, upon the number you intend to send). Never photocopy. No-one is impressed by a circular. Make the employer think you've made a special effort.

Always be precise and to the point. If you've already jotted down your own details under the headings given you may think it will be difficult to fit everything on to just two or three sides. You must! Employers do not want to read page after page of endless details. Be ruthless. Take your material and cut out everything except the key points which are relevant to this application. Keep it short and sweet.

Make sure the C.V. is easy to understand. Avoid technical phrases, jargon or slang. The employer may not understand what you mean. He may also think you're showing off. Use short, simple phrases and explanations which everyone can understand.

You should never exaggerate or lie. You should, of course, jiggle the facts so that they are seen in the best light, but outright deceit is not only wrong but may backfire. You may have to prove you *do* have the qualifications you claim or you may get the job on the basis of a job you never actually held. You may then find yourself dismissed and out of work. What happens then?

You should also remember that a curriculum vitae can, if you wish, be compiled in different ways under different headings. There is no right or wrong way. You do not need to adhere rigidly to the headings given here. Adjust them to suit your own circumstances. Remember that you are trying to promote your best points.

There are a number of employment agencies who will draw up a C.V. for you. It will look very professional. Check out agencies in your area, see what they offer and at what price. It can be a worthwhile investment.

Take care when compiling your C.V. if you do it yourself. Keep writing and re-writing it until you're happy. Then show it to a friend or colleague. If they were the employer, would they employ you? Be prepared to listen to criticism and adjust your C.V. accordingly. Don't stop working on it until you're absolutely satisfied it's the best you can do. Then, and only then, should you submit it.

COMPILATION

Personal Details

As indicated, a curriculum vitae can be divided into four main areas. The PERSONAL DETAILS section is easy to complete. Type your full name and current address. If appropriate, note both your home and work telephone number. A daytime work number can be helpful if an employer wants to call you in for an interview at short notice. Alternatively, just give your home phone number and prime your partner in case of a phone call (refer to Chapter Five: Using the Telephone).

You should then note your age and/or date of birth. Following this you would normally detail your marital status (single/engaged/married/divorced or widowed) and your dependants. Some people indicate you should state your nationality too.

Clearly these points are easy for you to complete. However, it is an unfortunate fact that, despite the large number of anti-discrimination laws passed, discrimination still exists amongst certain employers. There is no point in pretending otherwise. If you feel you are applying for a job where you could potentially be discriminated against because you are, say, a woman who is married with children, then you may be advised to omit 'marital status' and 'dependants' from your C.V. After all, these facts should have no bearing on your ability to do the job. If you did include the details and were rejected, you would never really know if it was because of that. Of course, you could never prove it either.

If you omit these (often irrelevant) details and then have an interview when the points are raised you may then, if rejected, be able to judge if it was because of discrimination. In theory, of course, you should not need to think about such points. In practice, unfortunately, you do. (There are a number of books specifically designed for women job hunters. These are detailed in the bibliography at the back of this book.)

An example of a completed PERSONAL DETAILS section of a C.V.

PERSONAL DETAILS

NAME:	ANTHONY JOHN HAYES
ADDRESS:	12 BEAUMONT PARK, THRETFORD, SURREY
TELEPHONE NUMBER:	(0446) 9219
AGE:	27

DATE OF BIRTH: 7 SEPTEMBER 1961

DEPENDANTS: NONE

Of course, it is not always necessary to use the words PERSONAL DETAILS and NAME, ADDRESS and so on. It is a personal choice. For example, the following layout, bearing in mind previous comments, is as good.

PERSONAL DETAILS

MAUREEN SEABROOK.
45 WOODTHORPE VIEW, THRETFORD, SURREY
(0446) 9210
36 YEARS OLD

You must, of course, decide for yourself how you lay out your C.V. and what it contains.

Education

State, firstly, the schools you have attended from the age of eleven. An employer is unlikely to be interested in any schools before that age. You should also give dates. For example:
SCHOOLS: FULLBROOK SECONDARY SCHOOL SEPTEMBER 1982–JUNE 1989
If the school was in a different area and, therefore, unfamiliar to the employer you should also state its location. For example:
SCHOOLS: FULLBROOK SECONDARY SCHOOL, ROPE WALK, MIDDLE-TON, HANTS SEPTEMBER 1982–JUNE 1989
If you have attended a number of schools you would, for example, state:
SCHOOLS: FULLBROOK SECONDARY SCHOOL, ROPE WALK, MIDDLE-TON, HANTS SEPTEMBER 1982–APRIL 1984. COOMBE SEC-ONDARY SCHOOL, RYDENS ROAD, GREENDALE, SUFFOLK APRIL 1984–JUNE 1986.
WOODHAM MANOR SECONDARY SCHOOL, RANLEIGH ROAD, WOOD-HAM MANOR, BUCKS SEPTEMBER 1986–JUNE 1989.
You should comment on the reasons why you have attended

several schools even if you feel the reason is obvious. The employer is not to know, for example, that your father was moved around the country by his company. The employer may think you had been expelled. Add a brief note after the final schools' details. Alternatively, add an asterisk indicating a footnote at the end of the C.V. or a comment in the supporting letter. Keep the comment short and concise.

For example

My father was promoted by his company to different posts around the country.

You should also add:

We have now settled permanently in this area.

After all, the employer must be convinced that you are here to stay. Employees are partly chosen on the basis that they are a good, long-term promotion prospect. Rightly or wrongly, you probably won't get the job if he thinks you'll be moving again soon.

Following on from SCHOOLS you would, if applicable, detail colleges and universities in the same way. For example:

DOWNLAND SIXTH FORM COLLEGE, STARRETT ROAD, DOWNLAND, SUSSEX SEPTEMBER 1985–JUNE 1987.

BEESTON POLYTECHNIC, PENHRYN ROAD, BEESTON, DEVON SEPTEMBER 1987–JUNE 1989.

QUALIFICATIONS is the next heading. State firstly the qualification – GCSE, O Level, A Level, HNC, HND, Degree and so on. Some texts indicate that you should detail your highest qualification first and work downwards. However it is better if you start with the lowest qualification and work upwards. The last qualification the employer reads will then be your best.

Following this, state your subjects and their grades. If you do not it may be assumed that you did not do as well as you actually did. Put down the dates when you passed each exam. If, for example, you sat Mathematics and English language 'O' levels in the fourth year it will indicate that you are brighter than the majority in those important subjects.

Finally, state the examining bodies.
An example of this section could be:

QUALIFICATIONS

'O' level Mathematics	Grade 'C'	June 1984	Associated Exam. Board
'O' level English Language	Grade 'C'	June 1984	Associated Exam. Board
'O' level Statistics	Grade 'C'	June 1985	Associated Exam. Board
'O' level Physics	Grade 'C'	June 1985	Associated Exam. Board
'O' level Chemistry	Grade 'B'	June 1985	Associated Exam. Board
'O' level Biology	Grade 'B'	June 1985	Associated Exam. Board
'O' level English Literature	Grade 'A'	June 1985	Associated Exam. Board
'O' level History	Grade 'A'	June 1985	Associated Exam. Board
'O' level French	Grade 'A'	June 1985	Associated Exam. Board
'O' level German	Grade 'A'	June 1985	Associated Exam. Board
'A' level Physics	Grade 'B'	June 1987	Associated Exam. Board
'A' level Chemistry	Grade 'B'	June 1987	Associated Exam. Board
'A' level Biology	Grade 'A'	June 1987	Associated Exam. Board

Generally, you should not include details of exams for which you obtained a grade below the accepted 'pass' level. Do not highlight your failures. If, of course, you believe you failed for a particular reason (a death in the family or a road accident affected your performance) you could add and state:

I was involved in a road accident prior to this examination.

and perhaps add

. . . I intend to re-sit this exam next June.

This would show you in a good light.

If you have studied subjects which were never designed to lead to examinations then these could be stated. For example:

QUALIFICATIONS

'O' level English Language	Grade 'C'	June 1986	Associated Exam. Board
'O' level History	Grade 'B'	June 1986	Associated Exam. Board
'O' level Geography	Grade 'B'	June 1986	Associated Exam. Board

I also studied 'Religious Education', 'Home Economics' and 'Childcare' which were non-exam subjects in our school.

In this instance it indicates that you have outside interests and are interested in subjects other than those which lead purely to examinations. It indicates you enjoy learning.

Many employers will accept your qualifications without checking to see if they are correct. As a result some job hunters lie, especially if their real qualifications are poor. You should, of course, stick to the truth. You may feel that, with four GCSE's, you will be less likely to succeed than the applicant with eight GCSE's. This need not necessarily be true. Employers look for more than just qualifications, otherwise why bother to interview? They could simply pick the applicant with the most GCSE's or the best 'A' level or degree results. It may be that your four GCSE's were achieved through evening classes and, perhaps, you're now studying for a further two. That shows initiative, hard work and dedication. That is impressive.

I remember interviewing one applicant for a job whose qualifications and experience were good and, more importantly, his personality was just right. I thought he would fit into the team well. Then I asked to see his certificates. He couldn't show me any. If he'd been honest from the start I would have employed him anyway but, not surprisingly, changed my mind. Who wants to employ a liar? Don't let anything like this happen to you.

You should also state your ACTIVITIES other than academic at school, college or university. This is an important point. As stated, employers look beyond basic qualifications when choosing an employee. They want to know what type of person you are. Are you a cold automaton that simply does the job and no more or a team member who will slot in and work well with colleagues? Your activities and interests at school or college may give the employer some clues. For example, look at the following entries on C.V's I have received. Rightly or wrongly what is your immediate reaction to each? What type of person do you see in your mind?

82

ACTIVITIES: I HAD NO TIME FOR OUTSIDE INTERESTS AT UNIVERSITY.

ACTIVITIES: AT SCHOOL AND UNIVERSITY, I WAS IN THE TENNIS AND SWIMMING TEAMS.

ACTIVITIES: I PLAYED BRIDGE AND CHESS AT UNIVERSITY AND WAS A MEMBER OF BOTH UNIVERSITY TEAMS.

Which would you prefer to employ? It depends, of course, on the job, but few employers would want the first applicant even if he had an excellent degree to support his rather sharp and pompous statement. What sort of person has absolutely no other interests apart from passing a degree? He may be motivated but perhaps it is to the point of obsession. The other two are both probably wildly different types, but both show outside interests and are members of teams which is a very important point.

It does no harm incidentally to add a comment about specific achievements at this point.

Do remember though to keep any comments precise. A C.V. is a *précis* of your life not a full scale autobiography.

For example:

ACTIVITIES: I PLAYED BRIDGE AND CHESS AT UNIVERSITY. I WAS A MEMBER OF BOTH UNIVERSITY TEAMS. WE WERE REGIONAL CHESS CHAMPIONS EACH YEAR I WAS ON THE TEAM.

Or:

ACTIVITIES: I WAS A KEEN CROSS COUNTRY RUNNER AT SCHOOL AND WAS SCHOOL CHAMPION FOR TWO YEARS. I ALSO RAN FOR THE SCHOOL TEAM IN THE REGIONAL CHAMPIONSHIPS.

Linked to ACTIVITIES are POSTS OF RESPONSIBILITY. Again, try to think of some post you have held. If you cannot think of anything leave it out. Be flexible. Remember that an employer is generally looking for staff who show qualities such as responsibility, dependability and trustworthiness. If you were a prefect or head boy or girl then that may indicate such qualities.

For example:

POSTS OF RESPONSIBILITY: NONE.
POSTS OF RESPONSIBILITY: HEAD LIBRARIAN
POSTS OF RESPONSIBILITY: CLASS PREFECT.
POSTS OF RESPONSIBILITY: CLASS REGISTER
                              COLLECTOR.

Remember, at this point, that every curriculum vitae is different but the aim is always the same: to highlight your strengths and disguise your weaknesses. You must, therefore, be adaptable when you compile yours. The applicant who completed the first C.V. and stated POSTS OF RESPONSIBILITY: None, has rigidly stuck to the framework when, clearly, it could be to his disadvantage. He should simply have left this out. Similarly the applicant who stated that he was the 'Class register collector' should have left the section out too. This really was written on one C.V. by a young man who had obviously racked his brains to think of some responsibility he'd had at school. Unfortunately collecting the class register from the staff room is on par with being 'milk monitor'! So, be sensible. If you haven't actually had any significant posts of responsibility leave it out completely.

Experience

Even if you are applying for your first job it is important that you indicate some sort of relevant experience in a Saturday, holiday or evening job. If you've worked on a voluntary basis this would be worth mentioning as well. You would certainly be considered favourably if you had helped in, for example, a charity shop or an old peoples' home. Similarly, you would be viewed in a good light if you'd obtained work from your own efforts. You may, perhaps, have started a car cleaning service. Mention it even if you think it has no relevance to this job. It has. It shows initiative. If you have been employed you need, as shown, to detail the name of the organisation, its location, your job title, dates of employment, duties and, most importantly, your reasons for leaving.

As said already, some texts state you should start with your current or most recent job and work backwards. I recommend that you start with your first job and work forwards. The employer will then read about your current job last.

State the organisation and its location. For example:

BOOTS, THE ARCADE, DEEPDALE, NORTHUMBERLAND.

If the organisation is likely to be unfamiliar to the prospective employer then offer a brief explanation. For example:

BARHAM AND BROWN (PHOTOGRAPHIC STUDIO), GROVE LANE, SHEERWATER, NORFOLK.

Never assume that the employer knows the organisation.

State your 'Job Title'. As indicated in 'Preparation', keep it simple and easy to understand. Avoid any fancy titles you may have been given by your last company. Use the simplest title you can think of that everyone can understand. Following this you should add your employment dates and detail your main duties. As always keep this brief and succinct. For example:

EXPERIENCE
ORGANISATION: GREGORY AND DAVISON (HARDWARE STORE), HAMILTON ROAD, THRETFORD, SURREY

JOB TITLE: SALES ASSISTANT (JUNE 1987– APRIL 1989)

DUTIES: I SOLD STOCK OVER THE COUNTER. I ORDERED GOODS FROM OUR SUPPLIERS. I WAS IN CHARGE OF THE STOCK ROOM AND WAS RESPONSIBLE FOR MAINTAINING GOOD STOCK LEVELS.

Clearly, this employee has mentioned his responsibilities too. This has the benefit of showing he could be trusted and was reliable and dependable.

Or:

EXPERIENCE
- UNDERTOWN COLLEGE OF HIGHER AND
  FURTHER EDUCATION, BROWNLOW ROAD,
  UNDERTOWN, SURREY
- LECTURER (SEPTEMBER 1988–JUNE 1989)
- I TAUGHT BUSINESS STUDIES AND ECONOMICS
  AT GCSE AND 'A' LEVEL.

This applicant could, if he had thought a little more, have added:

I WAS RESPONSIBLE FOR SETTING AND MARKING
COURSE ASSESSED WORK. I WAS ALSO RESPONSIBLE
FOR SETTING MOCK EXAMINATIONS.

You do need to keep plugging away modestly at your achievements as well; after all, if you don't, no-one else will.

For example, the employee at Gregory and Davison could have added:

SALES ACROSS THE COUNTER DOUBLED WHILST I
WAS THERE. I WAS 'SALESMAN OF THE YEAR' LAST
YEAR.

The employee at Undertown College could have added;

67% OF MY STUDENTS – COMPARED TO A 42%
NATIONAL AVERAGE – PASSED THEIR EXAMS WITH
A 'C' GRADE OR HIGHER.

You should finally state your reasons for leaving. This is very important. There are a number of 'good' reasons for leaving such as 'I left because . . .

'I wanted to progress with my career.' (Showing ambition.)

'The Company is re-locating and I have roots in this area.' (Showing you are dependable, reliable and a good, long-term prospect.)

'I felt I had achieved all I could within a small company.' (Showing ambition.)

'I wanted to move to this area for my family . . . better environment/better schools/close to parents.' (Showing you are here to stay and care about your family too.)

'The job did not challenge me enough.' (Showing ambition.)

Always think carefully before you state your reasons. How will they be interpreted by the prospective employer?

'Bad' reasons for leaving include:

'I didn't get on with the boss/my colleagues.' (It indicates you may not fit in here either.)

'I fancied doing something different.' (It indicates you're rather changeable and may fancy another change soon.)

'I was turned down for promotion.' (It indicates you might be unpromotable.)

'I was dismissed.' If you were sacked, for whatever reason, you should try to avoid stating this fact. It never looks good. However, you may have little choice but to state it if you were dismissed from your last job. Obviously, your prospective employer will expect a reference from that last employer. (If you were sacked, it may be worthwhile, before applying for a new job, to write to your old employer to see if you can persuade him to give you a reasonable reference. He may do. It's worth a try. If he refuses you should come clean with a prospective employer.)

I would avoid stating that you were dismissed when compiling your C.V. though. Omit the 'reason for leaving'. You may then get the chance to explain face to face. Be honest. If you deserved to be sacked admit it but show you have learned your lesson. Everybody is entitled to one mistake. If you think your dismissal was unreasonable you can explain your reasons in a clear, logical manner. Show you are mature and responsible and you may get the interviewer on your side.

An example of this section on 'Experience' could read:

EXPERIENCE

KALEIDOSCOPE (BABY SHOP), TREETOPS SHOPPING CENTRE, THRETFORD, SURREY
SALES ASSISTANT (JUNE 1982–JUNE 1986)
MY DUTIES INCLUDED SELLING BABY CLOTHES AND NURSERY GOODS. I WAS RESPONSIBLE FOR DELIVERING GOODS TO CUSTOMERS AROUND THRETFORD. I HELPED TO INTRODUCE A NAPPY DELIVERY SERVICE WHICH BECAME THE MOST PROFITABLE PART OF THE BUSINESS.
I LEFT TO PROGRESS WITH MY CAREER.

BABYTIME (BABY SHOP) 70 THE HIGH STREET, BRANDON, SURREY
SHOP MANAGER (JUNE 1986–)
I AM WHOLLY RESPONSIBLE FOR ALL ASPECTS OF SHOP MANAGEMENT. I HAVE HELPED (. . . this always shows you are modest) TO DOUBLE SALES SINCE I TOOK OVER.
I WISH TO LEAVE 'BABYTIME' TO BECOME REGIONAL MAN-AGER WITH YOUR ORGANISATION.

To further assist you in compiling a curriculum vitae, here is another example of a completed C.V.

CURRICULUM VITAE

PERSONAL DETAILS:
– SUSAN JONES
– 50 BRIGHTWELL CLOSE, THRETFORD, SURREY KP17 4LF
– (0446) 9292
– 17 YEARS OLD

EDUCATION:
– THRETFORD SECONDARY SCHOOL, 17 ABBEY ROAD, THRETFORD, SURREY
– SEPTEMBER 1984 TO JUNE 1989

GCSE HISTORY	GRADE 'C'	JUNE 1989
GCSE GEOGRAPHY	GRADE 'C'	JUNE 1989
GCSE MATHEMATICS	GRADE 'A'	JUNE 1989
GCSE ENGLISH LANGUAGE	GRADE 'A'	JUNE 1989
GCSE OFFICE SKILLS	GRADE 'A'	JUNE 1989

– I AM ALSO, AT PRESENT, STUDYING FRENCH AND GERMAN AT NIGHT SCHOOL. I WILL BE SITTING GCSE EXAMS IN THESE SUBJECTS NEXT JUNE.

EXPERIENCE:
– BRIGHTWELLS FACTORY, BRIGHTWELL INDUSTRIAL ESTATE, BRIGHTWELL ROAD, THRETFORD, SURREY (MANUFACTURERS OF INDUSTRIAL AND COMMERCIAL LIGHTING EQUIPMENT).
– PART-TIME OFFICE JUNIOR DURING SCHOOL HOLIDAYS
– JULY 1986–
– I WORK IN THE OFFICE OF THE ABOVE FACTORY. I ANSWER THE PHONE, TAKE MESSAGES, TYPE LETTERS AND RUN GENERAL ERRANDS.

LEISURE INTERESTS:
I AM A MEMBER AND SECRETARY OF THE THRETFORD

'SCRABBLE' TEAM WHICH I HELPED TO START. WE ALSO
SET UP A LEAGUE FOR OTHER LOCAL TEAMS TO JOIN. WE
MEET AND PLAY EVERY WEEKEND. OUR TEAM REACHED
THE NATIONAL FINALS LAST YEAR.

As you will see Susan has varied her layout a little from the
suggested layout. This is a matter of personal choice. The result-
ing C.V. is rather brisk and businesslike and should be
accompanied with a friendlier letter. (Refer to 'Supporting Letters' in Chapter Four.)

CHAPTER FOUR

WRITING LETTERS

COMPOSING A LETTER
- LAYOUT
- STYLE

SUPPORTING LETTERS

LETTERS OF APPLICATION

'ON SPEC' LETTERS

CHAPTER FOUR

WRITING LETTERS

You may need to write many letters when you are job hunting. Before you write any though it is important that you know the basic 'rules' of letter writing.

COMPOSING A LETTER

Layout

The layout of a letter will vary from company to company and if you look at letters you have received you will see, for example, that the address may be across the top of the page or on the left or right side. Similarly, the date may be on the left or right and paragraphs may start at the left had margin or slightly inwards of it. Clearly, therefore, there is no right or wrong way of laying out a letter. It is a matter of personal choice. However, the most common and convenient layout is where every 'entry' starts on the left of the page and each paragraph starts from the left hand margin. This is the easiest layout to remember and it will look neat and businesslike even if you are writing the letter by hand. A business letter should consist of these 'entries' in the following order:

Your address
Your telephone number

Your reference
Our reference

Date

Name of person you are writing to
Their address

Greeting

(Subject)

Paragraph one
Paragraph two
Paragraph three (etc..)

Complimentary close
Signature
Your name
(Enclosures)
(Copies being sent to)

Leave a margin of perhaps one inch on A4 paper which you should keep all the way down the page and then, as indicated, start the letter with your address and telephone number at the top right hand side. Remember to print your address if it is complicated and could be misread.

Following this you may need to insert reference numbers. If you have received, for example, a letter inviting you in for an interview you should check to see if a reference was given in it. Look for 'Our ref:' This will normally consist of the initials of the letter writer followed by the initials of the typist. Therefore, if Peter Allen had dictated a letter to his secretary Maureen Browning it would appear as:

Our ref: PA/MB
It could also have a reference number if the correspondence is being kept on file. For example
Our ref: PA/MB 731.

If, therefore, appropriate you should put their reference under 'Your reference' in your reply. Some job hunters also put an 'Our reference' in their letters because they think it makes them look businesslike and professional. It doesn't. It looks pompous and pretentious on a job hunters' letter. Put 'Your reference' only if it is appropriate. If not, leave this section out completely.

Following this, leave a slight gap and add the date of the letter. For example

23 October 1988
17 April 1989
2 June 1989

You do not need to add 'rd', 'th' or 'nd' after 23, 17 or 2. Do not abbreviate the month to 'Oct', 'Apr', 'Jun' or year to '88 or '89. Avoid 23/10/88 or 17–4–89 as well.

Leave another slight gap after the date and, still adhering tightly to that invisible left hand margin, insert the recipient's title and address. For example:

The Personnel Manager
Gayther and Sanderson Ltd
Thretford Industrial Park
Valley Road
Thretford, Surrey KP17 4LP

If you can discover the personnel manager's name (as you should) then you could put:

Mr A M Reynolds
Gayther and Sanderson Ltd
Thretford Industrial Park
Valley Road
Thretford, Surrey KP17 4LP

You could, if you wish, also add 'The Personnel Manager' between 'Mr A M Reynolds' and 'Gayther and Sanderson Ltd'. This would be sensible if the personnel manager's name was fairly common (such as Smith or Jones) and the organisation was very large. It might then go to the wrong Mr Smith or

Miss Jones within the company. You would then start your letter with a greeting such as:

Dear Sir,
or
Dear Madam,

In theory, 'Sir' or 'Madam' is very formal and should be used when you have not met each other. However, if you're job hunting you should, of course, find out 'Sir' or 'Madam's' name and use it. Nowadays they would certainly not be offended and it shows you have done your homework. You would therefore put:

Dear Mr Reynolds
or
Dear Mrs Hammond
or
Dear Miss Hopkins

If you did not know if 'Madam' was a 'Mrs' or a 'Miss' you would write:

Dear Ms Hammond,
or
Dear Ms Hopkins,

Following this you could note the 'Subject' you are writing about. For example:

Dear Mr Reynolds,
Re: SALES ASSISTANT VACANCY (M17)
or
Dear Ms Hammond
re: JOB VACANCIES

Include a 'Subject' heading if you feel it is appropriate. It can be useful. It immediately tells the reader what the letter is about without her having to read it all to find out.

Moving on you would then write the letter with each paragraph starting tightly against your invisible margin. (The actual contents of each paragraph will be discussed further on in this chapter.)

You would conclude the letter with 'Yours faithfully' if your greeting was 'Dear Sir' or 'Dear Madam'. Alternatively you would close with 'Yours sincerely' if your greeting was 'Dear Mr Reynolds', 'Dear Mrs Hammond' or 'Dear Miss Hopkins'. Sign your name. It looks careless and unprofessional if you do not. Make your signature readable. No-one is impressed by a flashy signature. It looks pretentious. Below your signature print your name.

With some letters you might enclose samples of your work, photocopies of certificates (never send originals) or the names and addresses of referees. If you do this, leave a small gap after your printed name and add 'enc' or 'encs' which would indicate an enclosure or enclosures. Attach any enclosures to the letter with a paper clip so they will not become detached. If you had sent a copy of the letter elsewhere you would then add, below 'encs', the phrase:

Copy to Mr Brown

or

Copies to Mr Brown and Mrs Porterfield

If your letter needs to run on to a second or even third page you would simply write or type the following at the top of the page along your invisible left hand margin.

2
23 October 1988
Mr Reynolds

or

3
17 April 1989
Mrs Hammond

or

4
2 June 1989
Miss Hopkins

Then carry on with the letter.
Overall your letter would therefore look something like this:

13 Shortley Road
Thretford, Surrey KP17 8NG
(0446) 9299

Your ref: AMR/IM

17 September 1989

Mr A M Reynolds
Gayther and Sanderson Ltd
Thretford Industrial Park
Valley Road
Thretford, Surrey KP17 4LP

Dear Mr REYNOLDS,
re: INTERVIEW FOR TRAINEE MANAGER VACANCY
Paragraph one . . .
Paragraph two . . .
Paragraph three . . .
Yours sincerely,

Michael James

M. JAMES

Style

You now know the basic 'rules' of laying out a letter. It is now
important to consider the style of a letter.

Firstly, your letter must, of course, look professional. Choose
good quality, A4 business paper and matching envelopes. No

employer will be impressed by a scrappy piece of lined paper from a pad purchased at a supermarket. Be professional.

Unless the job advertisement indicates otherwise you should always have your letters typed. Look in newsagents' windows and you'll often find advertisements from, perhaps, housewives who do typing for a relatively low price. Alternatively write the letter carefully by hand. Be neat. Choose a good quality fountain pen rather than a cheap throwaway one. This letter is your advertisement. You are selling yourself. Make it look classy.

Never send a photocopied letter even if you are writing many 'on spec'. Always write a personal letter to a named individual. No employer will be impressed by a letter that's obviously been circulated to dozens of potential employers. You might as well save yourself the price of a stamp and not sent it at all.

Every letter should be relatively brief. Be direct and to the point. Don't ramble on trying to emphasise a particular quality. State what you have to say and then move on. Avoid irrelevance. The fact that you were a marvellous rugby player at university may, perhaps, be worth mentioning if the job involves you working as a team member and the company is proud of its sports teams. It may help you. However, if you are applying for a job as a freelance market researcher where you would work on your own then it would be irrelevant to your application.

Every letter should convey a sense of enthusiasm for the job. Show them you are keen. Think about the words you use. For example, phrases such as 'I felt I must write immediately', 'I relish the type of challenge your job offers' and 'this excellent opportunity . . .' convey a lively and dynamic attitude.

Try to write in a simple style. Avoid long, complicated or technical words and phrases. A letter should be easy to read and understand. Keep words, sentences and paragraphs short and snappy.

Make sure the letter is logical. Before you write it read the advertisement, job description or specifications again. Take a sheet of blank paper. Jot down on one side what the employer wants and, on the other, what you can offer. Plan the letter out and decide what points you are going to raise where. Although this is dealt with in more detail in the following sections, you would normally write a letter in the following, logical order:

The opening paragraph should indicate the reason and purpose of the letter. If applicable you would start by acknowledging any previous correspondence and continue by stating why you have written. For example:

> Thank you for your letter of 13 July 1989 inviting me for an interview. I write to confirm that I will be delighted to attend at 2.30 pm on 20 July at your head office.

Alternatively:

> I have read your advertisement in today's 'Daily Telegraph' for a freelance researcher. I wish to apply for this vacancy and enclose my curriculum vitae for your attention.

The middle paragraphs should logically develop the letter in a clear, concise way. Each paragraph should deal with a separate topic. If you were writing, for example, a letter to support your curriculum vitae or application form, you might deal with your education in one paragraph followed by your qualifications, work experience and leisure interests.

The concluding paragraph may, if it is a long letter of application, briefly summarise the points you have raised. It should then state the action that you expect the recipient to take. For example:

> I look forward to hearing from you in due course to arrange an interview to discuss the vacancy further.

or

> I hope you will feel able to offer me an interview. Perhaps you would like to ask your secretary to telephone me on the above number to discuss a convenient time.

When you've written the letter put it to one side for an hour or two. Then look at it again. Have you laid it out correctly?

Is it brief, enthusiastic, well written and logical? Have you put across all the points you wanted to make?

Check your spelling carefully. Consider your punctuation and grammar. If you've made any mistake, however slight, always re-do the entire letter. It must be perfect. Your future could depend on it. No employer will be impressed by a typewritten letter which, when held to the light, has dozens of Tipp-ex marks. No employer will be impressed by handwritten letters where words are scratched out or 'a's turned to 'o's or 'n's turned to 'm's.

Show your letter to a friend or colleague. What is their honest opinion? Listen to criticism. Act on it. Re-write if necessary.

When you're happy with your letter, take a copy for your file. Always keep copies of all correspondence as you may want to refer to them again.

Fold the letter carefully. It should look neat when it is removed from the envelope. Instead of folding it in half and half again, fold the bottom third of the page upwards and the top third downwards. When it is opened there will then be two rather than three folded lines across the page. This looks better.

Type or write the recipient's name and address carefully in the centre of the envelope. Fix the stamp neatly and, of course, send your letter by first class post.

You may think many of these tips are rather petty and on their own they are. You should, however, remember that you are trying to convey a good image and all these little points help you to succeed in this aim.

SUPPORTING LETTERS

Many employers ask applicants to either send in a curriculum vitae or to complete an application form. **These must always be accompanied by a supporting letter**. Such a letter has a very important role to play and can have a significant effect on the success of your application. Some applicants return, for example, an application form with a letter like this:

> Dear Sir (. . . no name?)
> I am pleased to enclose my application form for your attention (. . . which is rather obvious).
> Yours sincerely   (. . . which should be faithfully)
>   (..no signature?)
> B J Baxter

This is woefully inadequate. A supporting letter must highlight your key strengths (as indicated in your C.V. or application form) and link them up to the employer's requirements. Many C.V.'s and all application forms will be similarly laid out and it can be difficult to make yours stand out from the crowd. This, therefore, is the purpose of the supporting letter.

Gordon Lukins is a sales representative for a small wholesalers of office equipment. Gordon is looking for another job because the wholesalers are in financial trouble. He sees an advertisement in a trade magazine from a leading office equipment manufacturer. They require a new sales representative. Gordon applies for the job.

> Dear Mr Pengelly
> re: SALES REPRESENTATIVE VACANCY (S3)
> I read your advertisement for the above vacancy in this month's 'Office Equipment News' published today. I enclose my curriculum vitae for your attention.
>
> As you will see I am an experienced sales representative in the trade having worked for an office equipment wholesalers for the past five years. I am, of course, already very familiar with your company and products.
>   I note from your advertisement that the successful applicant will cover the South of England and will be responsible for servicing existing accounts and generating new ones. I already cover this territory. At present I service 125 accounts. The company had 48 accounts when I joined them.
>   I very much want to work for Bradley and Derham because, as stated in your advertisment, you are a dynamic, go ahead

company. I also believe this job offers me the exciting challenge
I am looking for.

I look forward to meeting you.

Yours sincerely

Gordon Lukins

Gordon Lukins

Enc

Gordon starts his supporting letter well by indicating the subject
of the letter and quoting a reference number. There can therefore
be no confusion about what job he is applying for.

His first paragraph is brief and direct. He states where he saw
the advertisement. He shows he's on the ball by adding 'published today'. He then draws Mr Pengelly's attention to the
attached C.V. (or application form).

In the second paragraph Gordon has correctly decided that
his main strength is his experience within the trade. He states
this simply. Similarly, it must be an advantage to know the
products already. Again, he states this.

He continues the theme of experience into the third paragraph
and links up his strengths with the employer's requirements.
He already covers the South of England. He services a significant number of accounts (many of which would already be
Bradley and Derhams customers too) and he shows he can
generate new business: 'I service 125 accounts. The company
had 48 accounts when I joined them.'

In the fourth paragraph he shows enthusiasm, repeating that
the company is 'dynamic' and 'go ahead' and that the vacancy
is an 'exciting challenge'.

Finally, he indicates he wants a meeting

The letter therefore is suitably brief and all the key points are
put across neatly. When Mr Pengelly reads the C.V. he will
already have a favourable impression of Gordon.

Of course you will be thinking that this is an easy letter
for Gordon to write. He is, on paper, a natural for the job.
Nevertheless Gordon has to tread a very careful path with this
letter. He has many strengths he could promote. He works in

the same trade. He is experienced and knows the business inside out. He knows Bradley and Derham well. He knows their products. He knows, in all probability, their customers. He may even know their staff including the representative who is leaving, and even Mr Pengelly himself.

Many applicants in this situation can easily fail. They are so ideal for the job that they feel they have to prove how good they are and write page after page of details to show their experience and knowledge. Alternatively, they become over-confident and assume they will get the job automatically. They don't take the application seriously. They do not bother to include a C.V. or application form and write a cocky, over familiar and boastful letter. Gordon, for example, could easily have written this letter.

Dear Stan,

Bill Laflan told me that Reg will be leaving shortly, so I thought I'd drop you a line to tell you that I would be interested in this job. I know that you are well acquainted with my work (you'll remember we had dinner a year ago) but I thought I should write anyway. I've been at Harpers now for five years. I've done very well but it's time to move on to a better company. I already cover the South of England and know all your customers very well. I've got 125 accounts which is about 50 more than Reg had so I reckon I can get you some new business pretty quick. I think we'd do well together. I'm down your way next week so perhaps I could call in then.

With best wishes

Gordon Lukins

This letter (and I have received many similar applications) does everything wrong: it is cocky, over familiar and boastful. It also criticises a current employer (which you should never do) and takes the job for granted. Finally, it is badly written, poorly laid out and confusing to read.

Be sensible when you write a supporting letter. It is, of course, important that you repeat key facts from the C.V. to emphasise your suitability, but don't labour the points endlessly or appear boastful.

LETTERS OF APPLICATION

Many advertisements will ask you to 'apply in writing'. You therefore have a choice. You can either send in a C.V. with a supporting letter (see 'Supporting Letters' and 'On Spec' letters) or, alternatively, send in just a letter of application. This letter should pick out the key strengths that would have been in your C.V. and develop them a little more fully than a supporting letter would.

Before writing such a letter look at the curriculum vitae framework on page 75. Jot down your details under the various headings of 'Personal Details', 'Education', 'Experience' and 'Leisure Interests'. Then ask yourself which details are your key strengths and which are relevant to this application. Cut out all those which are irrelevant. Your letter should be as succinct as possible.

Martin Rogers has seen an advertisement in the *Thretford Chronicle* for a trainee journalist on that paper. Applicants are invited to 'apply in writing to the Editor'. Martin drafts out a rough copy of a C.V. intending to send the C.V. with a supporting letter. He then decides to send just a letter. He wants to reply quickly and doesn't have time to draw up a C.V. neatly. In addition he wants to send samples of his work and these, with a C.V., would give the editor too much to read. Martin, therefore, eliminates all the details of the draft C.V. which he thinks are either weaknesses or irrelevant to this application and uses the remaining details to form the basis of the following letter.

Dear Mr Randall
re: TRAINEE JOURNALIST VACANCY (JV3)
I read of the above vacancy in your newspaper this morning and felt I must immediately write to apply for the job.

My name is Martin Rogers, I am nineteen years old and left Thretford Secondary school in June with the following qualifications.
GCSE ENGLISH LANGUAGE   (GRADE B)
GCSE ENGLISH LITERATURE   (GRADE B)

GCSE MATHEMATICS	(GRADE B)
GCSE BUSINESS STUDIES	(GRADE B)
GCSE FRENCH	(GRADE A)
GCSE GERMAN	(GRADE A)
GCSE SPANISH	(GRADE A)
'A'LEVEL ENGLISH LITERATURE	(GRADE B)
'A'LEVEL FRENCH	(GRADE B)
'A'LEVEL GERMAN	(GRADE B)

I also studied typing and shorthand at school. My speeds are currently 60 words per minute and 70 words per minute respectively. I am, at present practising both regularly and am improving all the time.

At school I also started and ran the school magazine *Bitz*. I edited this for two years. I enclose a copy of the last issue for your attention.

During the school holidays I worked for the *Brandon Bugle* as a researcher collecting and checking information for journalists. I also had a number of my own articles published and enclose a small selection. Although this work was on a voluntary basis, I chose to work the same hours as the employed staff because of the experience I would gain in local journalism.

I would very much like to meet you to tell you a little more about myself. I am available at any time and look forward to hearing from you. My phone number is Thretford 9200.

Yours sincerely

Martin Rogers

Martin Rogers

Encs

As you will note, Martin has kept very loosely to the C.V. framework, selecting and developing the key points within it. Looking at Martin's letter in more detail he starts well by referring to the editor by name and immediately identifies the vacancy. In the first paragraph he states where he saw the advertisement and that it was 'today'. He also shows enthusiasm: 'I must immediately write . . .'

In the second paragraph Martin gives his name and age. He does not mention (as detailed in the C.V. framework) his address and telephone number as these, of course, would be at the top of the page already. 'Date of Birth', 'Marital Status' and 'Dependants' are also irrelevant here. (In other circumstances they could be mentioned. If, for example, you were a woman with young children then these 'dependants' could be an advantage if you were applying for a job as a freelance journalist on a baby magazine.)

Martin then continues by naming the school he has just left. The editor of the *Thretford Chronicle* will obviously know Thretford Secondary School. He then details his qualifications which are both good and relevant. He also lays them out well. By breaking up the page with a list, he draws Mr Randall's attention to the qualifications and makes the page look more attractive as well. Martin mentions his typing and shorthand skills separately, thus emphasising them. These are, of course, his most relevant qualifications and a key strength. He also shows dedication by stating he is 'practising. . . . and improving all the time'.

Following this Martin mentions (in the next paragraph) his school activities which are again a key strength for this application. He encloses a copy of the magazine. This (he hopes) is impressive and will (as Martin correctly expected) carry far more weight than a C.V. would.

In the next paragraph Martin details his work experience which is highly relevant. He again encloses (good) samples of his work. He stresses that this work was unpaid but that he worked a full week for the experience. This indicates he is dedicated, hardworking and keen to learn. This, linked with his writing ability indicated in the work samples sent, should at least obtain an interview.

In the final paragraph Martin states what he wants and encourages action by giving Mr Randall his phone number.

'ON SPEC' LETTERS

'On spec' letters could perhaps have been included in the previous two sections. 'On spec' letters sent with C.V's are, in many ways, 'supporting letters' and those without C.V's are basically 'letters of application'. (You should therefore read the previous two sections if you intend to write 'on spec' letters). Nevertheless these letters should be considered separately. They play an important role in the job hunting process and are distinct from supporting letters and letters of application in that they are sent without reference to a specific vacancy.

Generally, it is sensible to send an 'on spec' letter with a carefully drawn up C.V. (refer to Chapter Three: Curricula Vitae). The 'on spec' letter would pick out the key points within the C.V. and link them up with the company's anticipated requirements. For example, Amanda Jones has just left Thretford Secondary School and is seeking a job as an office junior. She sees an article in the local paper that morning which indicates a firm of accountants is to open a new office in the town. She writes the following letter.

Dear Miss Hopkins

I read in this morning's 'Daily Echo' that your company, Brentwood and Snell, is opening a new office in Thretford next month. I am writing to ask if you have·any vacancies for office staff.

As you will note from the enclosed curriculum vitae, I already have experience of office work and duties. I have worked in the office at my father's factory for the past three years. Although this was on a part-time basis during school holidays, I did all the work expected of a full-time junior.

You will also note that I have obtained good qualifications in Mathematics, English Language and Office Skills which would help me in an office job. I am also studying French and German at evening classes. I think these could be of great benefit too if I worked for Brentwood and Snell. I know that you have offices in France and Germany.

In my spare time I enjoy games and competitions involving words or numbers. I am a member of the local Scrabble team and we even made the National Finals last year! We didn't win but it was great fun.

I do hope you might offer me an interview. I have included my telephone number (0446) 9292 – should you wish to telephone me. I would be very pleased to call and see you at any time convenient to you.

Yours sincerely

Amanda Jones

Amanda Jones

Enc

Amanda starts the letter well by saying 'Dear Miss Hopkins' rather than 'Dear Madam'. She has also put 'Miss' rather than 'Ms'. The article Amanda read either indicated Miss Hopkins was a 'Miss' or, alternatively, Amanda may have rung the company to find out.

The first paragraph is brief and succinct. Amanda states why she is writing. If Miss Hopkins doesn't have any vacancies or someone else is dealing with recruitment then she doesn't need to waste time reading further. Amanda also shows some other good touches. She read the article 'this morning' which shows she's on the ball. She writes 'your company' which will flatter Miss Hopkins who is probably an employee. She mentions the company 'Brentwood and Snell' which shows that the letter is individual rather than photocopied. She makes the enquiry specific to 'office staff' rather than just stating 'vacancies' which is too vague. At the same time she doesn't limit herself by being too specific and stating a particular job such as a 'secretary' or 'receptionist'.

The second paragraph immediately draws Miss Hopkins attention to Amanda's curriculum vitae. It continues by mentioning her key strength which is her experience. Obviously this experience was in her father's business and on a part-time basis. In case Miss Hopkins thinks this wasn't a proper job, Amanda specifically states she did 'all the work expected of a full-time junior'.

The third paragraph highlights another of Amanda's strengths which is her good, relevant qualifications for this job. She mentions evening classes which indicates she is hard-working and keen to get on. She then links the subjects French and

German to the job applied for by mentioning the company's overseas offices. This fact may have been mentioned in the article or perhaps Amanda has been doing her homework?

The fourth paragraph is included to show that Amanda has outside interests. After all, she has indicated that she works in an office in the school holidays and goes to evening school as well. She doesn't want to appear to be obsessive about work. She should be able to enjoy herself too. Nevertheless, her outside interests are still relevant to this application in that Scrabble involves, if you like, English and Maths. It's great fun too.

Amanda concludes with a brief paragraph showing that what she wants which is an interview. She also nudges Miss Hopkins into action by giving her phone number.

'On spec' letters can of course be sent without a C.V. As indicated in 'Letters of Application' such a letter should still be based around a C.V. framework. In reality the difference between an 'on spec' letter with or without a C.V. can be slight. If you look at the letter Amanda Jones sent with a C.V. it still follows a basic C.V. framework in that each paragraph looks separately at her 'experience', 'education' and 'leisure interests'. If she wanted to write a letter without a C.V. it could basically be the same although she would have to add a number of extra points from the C.V. which are important. She would, for example, need to state her qualifications and where her father's factory was. Other than that the difference is minimal although she could, if she wished, develop the key points more fully in just a letter.

Compare the following letter sent without a C.V. with the previous example.

Dear Miss Hopkins

I read in this morning's Daily Echo that your company, Brentwood and Snell, is opening a new office in Thretford next month. I am writing to ask if you have any vacancies for office staff.

My name is Amanda Jones, I am seventeen years old and have just left Thretford Secondary School where I obtained the following qualifications.

GCSE HISTORY	(GRADE C)
GCSE GEOGRAPHY	(GRADE C)
GCSE MATHEMATICS	(GRADE A)

GCSE ENGLISH LANGUAGE   (GRADE A)
GCSE OFFICE SKILLS   (GRADE A)

I think my Maths, English Language and Office Skills qualifications will help me in an office job. I am also studying French and German at evening classes which will be of benefit too. I know you have offices in France and Germany.

I already have experience of office work. My father owns the Brightwell factory in Thretford which manufactures lighting equipment and I have worked in the office there for the past three years.

In my spare time I enjoy games and competitions involving words or numbers. I am a member of the local Scrabble team and we made the National Finals last year! We didn't win, but it was great fun.

I do hope you might offer me an interview. I have included my phone number – (0446) 9292 – should you wish to telephone me. I would be delighted to call and see you at any time convenient to you.

Yours sincerely

Amanda Jones

Amanda Jones

Enc

Clearly, therefore it is up to you whether or not you send a C.V. with an 'on spec' letter.

CHAPTER FIVE

USING THE TELEPHONE

Having the confidence and ability to use the telephone is an important part of the job hunting process. You may wish to telephone a company 'on spec' or for an application form. You may be telephoned unexpectedly by a company to which you have applied inviting you in for an interview or, alternatively, even be interviewed on the telephone. As such, you need to prepare for a telephone conversation, know how to use your voice effectively and, of course, how to make a telephone call successfully.

PREPARATION

You may be one of the lucky few who can think on their feet and can handle any telephone conversation with style and confidence but, even so, a little preparation can still give you that extra sparkle.

It is, firstly, important that you are well organised. If you're going to make a phone call, do make sure that you can do it in a quiet room where you will not be interrupted. The television, screaming children or people talking in the background does not appear professional and, of course, could also distract you. If you cannot use the phone in a separate room or when the family is out, then you should consider telephoning from a phone box. Do make sure you have enough money and choose a telephone box which is rarely used. I recall telephoning one

115

prospective employer for an informal chat a few years ago. An elderly lady started to bang on the window because she felt she'd waited too long. Not surprisingly, I didn't get the job.

You should also prepare a list of points you want to mention during the conversation. If you know the extension number or the name of the person you want to speak to, then jot it down. Your mind may go blank when the phone is answered and you may fumble your words. I recall one young girl who once rang me for a discussion as suggested in our advertisements. I answered the phone and she asked to speak to Iain Johnson instead of me, Iain Maitland. Fortunately, she recovered quickly and explained that her boyfriend's name was Iain Johnson and she was used to ringing him at work. So, jot down the right name in big, capital letters.

It can also help, if you're nervous, to write down your opening few words. For example: 'Good morning, could you put me through to Mr Hutchinson on Extension 603 please . . . my name? Yes it's Michael James.'

You should also make a note of any reference numbers used in adverts or correspondence. In large organisations you may be speaking to a clerk in the personnel department. If, for example, you've rung for an application form, she may need to know the reference number so she can send you the correct form and job description.

Jot down, before the conversation, a list of your main strengths. Bring these into the conversation when you can. Keep your C.V. available as well so that you can refer to it. One of the problems with any telephone call or, of course, an interview, is drying up. You'll know that feeling when your mind goes blank. If you have all your relevant notes in front of you it always helps to avoid this happening.

You must also have a pen and separate sheet of paper to hand. Use it to jot down additional notes during the phone call. For example, if you are telephoning 'on spec' you may be asked to send in a C.V. for consideration. Make a note of the name of the person it should be sent to and their room number or department. If you manage to speak to the right person either 'on spec' or following an invitation to ring for an informal chat you should, similarly, note the date, time and location of any interview and, of course, the name of the interviewer.

If you're rung unexpectedly it is also important that you always keep a pen and paper by the phone. It creates a poor impression if you have to search for a pen and keep the prospective employer waiting. Buy a telephone message pad to leave by the phone in case you're out when an employer rings. Whoever answers the phone can simply fill it in.

Immediately before your phone call you must relax your voice. I am sure you have all experienced the situation, at one time or another, when you've been nervous, opened your mouth and a strangulated whisper came out. Limber up. Have a (non-alcoholic) drink to moisten your throat and lips. Breathe deeply. Sing a little!

Make sure you also feel relaxed in yourself. I always recall one applicant I spoke to on the phone. He started the conversation inaudibly and was clearly terrified throughout. At the end he actually said 'Hallo' instead of 'Goodbye' and put the phone down before I had finished speaking. Avoid this by practising. Get into the habit of regularly using the phone and having conversations. Practise mock phone calls with your partner or a colleague. After all, practice makes perfect.

After the phone call check you've made a note of all the important points. Then follow through. If you've arranged an interview you must start researching the job and company (see Chapter Six: 'Preparing for the Interview'). If you've been asked to send in a C.V. or samples of your work, then attend to these matters immediately. It shows efficiency and enthusiasm.

USING YOUR VOICE EFFECTIVELY

Your voice is very important. It is the key to a successful telephone call. It is, of course, equally important in an interview and, if you get the job, at work.

117

Your voice is a reflection of your personality. If you roll or slur your words and mumble the end of sentences the employer may think your work will be equally sloppy and half-hearted. If you speak with an affected voice the employer may think you are false.

You may also be judged on your accent. You would probably view a person with a South London accent differently from one with a Suffolk or West Midlands accent. You may think the slow, deliberate Suffolk drawl indicated a rather slow person. You may think the South London sharp talker was a con man. You would probably be wrong, but you do make instant judgments on a person's voice especially on the telephone. Bear it in mind.

If you feel depressed and unhappy it may also show in your voice. The employer may assume you will be miserable at work if you sound depressed and dull. If you sound nervous the employer may think you lack self confidence. Could you handle the job?

To succeed you must, firstly, speak clearly. Pronounce each word. Don't let your voice drop at the end of a sentence and fade away. Repeat key points. Spell out names. Repeat numbers. If you've rung 'on spec' the employer may be only half listening or may have distracting noises in the background. Don't let him mishear or misinterpret information.

Speak in your natural voice. There is no need to feel ashamed or embarrassed about it even if the employer speaks differently. You should, however, try to speak a little slower if you have a particularly strong accent and try to ease out any regional expressions that may not be understood.

You should, of course, also avoid using slang or clever technical expressions he or she may not understand. Never, of course, use bad language even if the employer does. Avoid annoying phrases such as 'you know', 'actually' and sentences that start 'I . . . I . . . I' all the time. It sounds self-centred and conceited. Try to keep your voice nice and steady. It shows you are a cool, calm person. Even if a question is unexpected try not to stumble or show you've been caught off balance. Avoid 'ums' and 'ers' or long silences when you've dried up. Always try to keep the conversation going.

118

Most people prefer to talk rather than listen. You must strike a careful balance. Try to speak as often as you can to show you are confident. At the same time don't waffle or be irrelevant. You've got a list of key points to get across. Make those points briefly and then shut up.

You must also listen to the employer. Hear what he or she says and indicate you're listening. In a face to face interview you would nod and smile. On the phone you must use the natural pauses in the conversation to indicate agreement – 'Yes' . . . 'mmm' . . . 'of course' . . . 'I agree' . . . 'that's very true' and so on.

When you practise conversations (as indicated in 'Preparation') you should consider taping them. Play them back and listen to your voice. How does it sound? Do you sound confident or nervous, lively or dull? Keep taping, listening and amending until you've ironed out all the imperfections you can. Don't worry if you hate the sound of your voice at first. Few people like their own voice. Improve yours with practice.

HOW TO WIN ON THE TELEPHONE

There are, of course, different situations whereby you might use the phone in job hunting. For convenience these situations have been divided into four sections. Do, however, read each one and consider how the points in each overlap with each other.

'On Spec' Calls

Instead of sending out 'on spec' letters, you may feel that you are better at speaking on the telephone. It is a personal choice. If you decide to ring 'on spec' you should be prepared. Before you telephone do think about your timing. As a general rule you should avoid telephoning between 9 and 10 a.m. The person you want to speak to may not yet be at their desk. Even if they are they may be busy opening the post or planning the day. He or she probably won't yet be on the ball. If you telephone between midday and two thirty they'll probably be at lunch. If you telephone after four they'll probably be thinking about going home. This 'timetable' isn't always true of course, but it can be. If you want to catch the employer at their best, you could try telephoning mid-morning. They will be into the swing of things and, with luck, you'll catch them at the right moment.

If you're telephoning a company you probably won't know who to speak to. You could ask to speak to the personnel manager or 'the person in charge of recruitment'.

Make your greeting bright and cheerful. Identify yourself. For example:

'Good morning, my name's Gordon Lukins. Could I speak to the personnel manager, please?'

Of course, some personnel managers will be busy. They may be used to 'on spec' calls and their staff may be told to put such callers off. The response could therefore be:

'Can you tell me what it's about?'

Clearly you are then at a disadvantage, having to explain yourself. You are on the defensive:

'Yes. I'm ringing to see if you've any jobs available.'
'I'm sorry but the personnel manager's very busy. He'd prefer it if you were to write in.'

Clearly, if you persevered you would cause bad feeling. Don't let this happen to you. Find out the personnel manager's name before the phone call. When you ring you should then say:

'Good morning, will you put me through to Mr Thompson, please. It's Mr Lukins calling'.

Referring to the personnel manager by name indicates you already know him. This is strengthened by stating who you are and the slightly authoritative instruction may mean you're put straight through. Even if the receptionist did query the call, you have started off on the right foot. Indicate Mr Thompson is expecting the call and that he knows who you are. You'll be put through.

Once you're through, many 'on spec' callers say:

'Good morning, can you tell me if you have any vacancies at the moment?'

This is too vague. If it's a large company there may be many vacancies. The personnel manager won't want to list them all. He won't know which are suitable for you. He doesn't even know who you are. You'll have started the conversation on the wrong foot.

Other applicants say:

'Good morning, are you free at the moment?'

Whether he is or not, you're inviting a 'No'. So don't say it. You must open strongly. Be polite. Identify yourself. Grab his attention.

For example:

'Good afternoon, Mr Thompson (it shows you're both on the ball and courteous). My name's Gordon Lukins. I'm an experienced salesman in the office equipment trade and wanted to talk to you about your company.'

Of course, no text can predict what the exact reply will be but you should at least avoid the conversation-killing word 'No'.

He may, of course, say:

'I'm sorry but I'm very busy now.'

You should not be disheartened. Keep going!

'Of course. I'm sorry to trouble you but it will only take a moment (don't pause here, just keep talking). Let me explain . . .'

121

Alternatively, he may perhaps reply:

'Oh really? What do you want to know?'

or:

'What sort of experience do you have?'

or:

'Who do you work for?'

At least you have a response and the ball is back in your court. Take your chance. You want him to offer you an interview for a job if one is available or to keep your details on file if not. Alternatively, you want to be put in touch with any other person or company who might have a suitable vacancy. Take two or three of your key strengths to seize his attention and generate interest. For example, in response to the last question you could say:

'I've been working for Harper and Sons for the last five years covering the South East (he needs to know the basic facts). I've been top salesman for the last three years (indicates your achievements) but I'm now looking for a new challenge (shows ambition) with a forward looking company like yours (which is flattering).'

You should then indicate what you want from him.

'I'd like to arrange an interview with you to discuss my future.'

Of course the response is unpredictable. It depends on the individual. However, the saying 'if you don't ask you don't get' is often true. He may be interested. If there is a vacancy he may invite you in or take the opportunity to ask you a series of questions to find out more about you. (Read 'Questions and Answers' in Chapter Seven for more details.)

He may, perhaps, turn you down:

'I'm very sorry but we've no vacancies at the moment.'

If you genuinely do want to work for this specific company you could reply:

'I appreciate that but I would still like to see you so that you might consider me if a vacancy arises in the future.'

He may agree.

Alternatively you could follow up the call with an 'on spec' letter (refer to 'On spec letters' on page 108). Then write regularly to refresh his memory. Many job hunters are successful by being in the right place at the right time. They do this by persevering. They get themselves into the position whereby their letter is opened just as a vacancy arises. So keep writing regularly.

If the personnel manager replied to your request for a meeting with:

'No I'm sorry, but there really is no point. There are no vacancies and I don't anticipate any in the future.'

Then you could ask:

'Fair enough, I'm sorry to have inconvenienced you. Could you tell me if you are aware of any similar vacancies in similar companies?' . . .

and then your job hunting process can start again.

'On spec' phone calls or letters *do* work. I have personally obtained each and every one of my jobs through an initial 'on spec' enquiry. The key to success is, as indicated, perseverance. Never give up. You may need to make hundreds of calls or send hundreds of letters to obtain even one interview but, one day, you will succeed.

Keep at it!

Telephoning for an application form

Clearly, this is a fairly simple telephone call, but do use the opportunity to find out as much background information as you can. As indicated, some companies send out job descriptions and even specifications with their application forms. When telephoning you should ask for them. Similarly you could ask for some information about the company or the interviewer (see Chapter Six: 'Preparing for the Interview').

The conversation could be:

'Good morning, (be bright and cheerful). I'm ringing with regard to the vacancy for trainee manager (always identify the post immediately; some applicants just ask for an application form but for what job?) Could you send me an application form, please?'

'Can you give me your name and address?'

'Yes, of course, it's Michael James J..A..M..E..S (always spell out the name. I've had post addressed to Mayland and Mattham instead of Maitland). My address is 13, one three, Shotley Road, that's S..H..O..T..L..E..Y. I live in Thretford, Surrey. That's T..H..R..E..T..F..O..R..D.

'That's fine. We'll get one in the post to you today.'

'Do you by chance have a job description or specification you could send me or some literature on the company? . . . I'd like to have a look through before I reply.'

'Yes, of course, I'll see what I can find.'

'Oh, by the way, could you also tell me the name of the person dealing with my application.' (this is very important).

'Yes, it'll be Mrs Brown, she's in charge of recruitment.'

'That's great, could you just give me her initials so I can address my reply to her?' (be thorough)

'Yes, it's Linda Brown . . .'

'That's fine. Thanks very much for your help. I do appreciate it (always be pleasant. The receptionist may be friendly with Mrs Brown and could comment on good or bad callers). You'll get the application form in the post to me today?'

'Yes I will.'

'Thanks again. Goodbye!

Of course, if you live nearby why not, as previously indicated, call in to collect the application form? This gives you a chance to have a look at the company and see if you want to work there. You might even get an on-the-spot interview. It's worth a try.

An Invitation to an Interview

After submitting a C.V. or application form you could be telephoned unexpectedly inviting you to come in for an interview. Such a phone call is not an opportunity to sell yourself. You've done that already in your application. Similarly it is not an interview. That comes later. The call should be brief and concise. For example:

'Thretford 9299' (always identify yourself with the phone number rather than saying 'Hallo').

'Good afternoon, this is Stevensons Bakery. May I speak to Mr James, please?'

'This is Michael James (Michael – or Mike – sound friendlier than Mr). What can I do for you?' (keep the conversation moving).

'I'm ringing about your application for the baker's job. Are you free to attend an interview tomorrow afternoon at two thirty?'

'Yes, of course. I'd be delighted (show enthusiasm). Can you tell me who's interviewing me and where?' (get the facts).

'Yes, I'll be interviewing you at the main factory. If you come to reception they'll bring you through to me.'

'That's fine . . . could I just take a note of your name, please?' (be sure to get all the facts).

'Mr Bartholomew. I'm the works manager.'

'Thank you, Mr Bartholomew, (show respect) I'll look forward to meeting you tomorrow afternoon at two thirty. Thank you very much for ringing.'

You must then jot down all the relevant points. You should then prepare for the interview (see Chapter Six: Preparing for the Interview).

The Telephone Interview

The job advertisement may ask you to telephone for an informal chat. Alternatively, you may be telephoned to discuss the job after sending in a letter, C.V. or application form. Both conversations are, in effect, a preliminary interview to weed out applicants.

All interviews, whether they are on the phone or 'face to face', are totally unpredictable. You could be asked questions on almost any subject that takes the interviewer's fancy. Therefore examples of telephone interviews will be of limited use. You should, however, be prepared. Read chapters six and seven before you ring the company for a chat or if you expect to be telephoned.

PREPARING FOR THE INTERVIEW

WAITING FOR A REPLY

RESEARCHING THE ORGANISATION

RESEARCHING THE JOB

RESEARCHING THE INTERVIEW

CHAPTER SIX

PREPARING FOR THE INTERVIEW

Once you've sent off your application form, curriculum vitae or letter you may feel inclined to sit back and wait for a reply. You may think that this is the only job you want, you're ideally qualified for it and you must at least be offered an interview.

KEEP LOOKING FOR WORK

You should, however, keep looking for work until you've actually got a job. There is no such thing as a certainty in job hunting.

You may not hear from a company for some time. You may think they've forgotten (which is very unlikely) or that they've rejected you but haven't had the courtesy to reply (which, unfortunately, is quite normal nowadays). Do not however chase the company for a reply. It makes you look desperate.

At some stage, of course, you will receive a reply. Often you will be rejected and examples of rejection letters are given on pages 137,139 and 174. Don't be too disheartened. There may have been hundreds of applicants for just one job. There's only one winner and, unfortunately, it wasn't you.

If you are job hunting you must accept that you will probably fail again and again before you finally succeed. It can take months, sometimes years. You must try to learn from your failures. Don't just screw up the letter in disgust and throw it in the waste paper basket. Take out all the details again. Look

129

at the advertisement, job description and specifications. Read through your application form, C.V. or letter of application. Did you make any obvious mistakes? In which areas were you weak? Can you see why you failed? You must recognise and, if possible, rectify your weaknesses.

Eventually, you will receive a letter inviting you in for an interview (examples are given on pages 140 and 141). Alternatively, you may be telephoned (see Chapter Five: 'Using the Telephone'). Study the letter carefully. Note the sex, initials and surname of the interviewer. Make sure you can pronounce the surname as you will want to greet the interviewer when you meet. If in doubt, telephone his or her secretary to check. Don't be embarrassed. It simply shows you're thorough.

You must also note the exact time and date of the interview. Don't be late and don't turn up on the wrong day as has sometimes happened. Note the location of the interview too. If any important points are unclear or have been omitted, ring up and check. Better to be safe than sorry.

You should, out of courtesy, then write to the interviewer to confirm that the time and place of the interview is convenient. It is, of course, important that you attend the interview as arranged unless it is absolutely impossible for you to do so. Interviews will normally all take place on one particular morning, afternoon or day and, generally, if you don't attend then you do not get a second chance (unless, of course, you had a genuine and important reason for missing it such as a funeral).

RESEARCHING THE ORGANISATION

You should, of course, already have found out about the organisation before you sent in your application form, curriculum vitae or letter. Before the interview it is important that you re-read any literature you have and, in addition, try to obtain any further information you can. To succeed in an interview you must show interest and enthusiasm, and a full knowledge of the company and its products or services will indicate these qualities to the interviewer. You will need to slip in comments to show you've done your homework.

The interviewer may also ask you questions such as 'What do you know about this company?', 'Tell me about our products' or 'What do you think of our competitors?' (See Chapter Seven: The Interview for further information on 'Questions and Answers'.) These questions offer you a marvellous opportunity to succeed if you have done your research. Clearly, you will almost certainly fail if you haven't. You may be able to think quickly but, in this situation, there can be no substitute for research.

Consider the following questions and make sure you comment on each during an interview;

- Who owns the organisation?
- What does the organisation do?
- What does the organisation sell?
- How does the organisation sell?
- How many outlets does it have?
- Where are they?
- How many employees does it have?
- Is it an expanding organisation?
- What is its reputation like?
- What are its strengths and weaknesses?
- Is the market expanding, static or diminishing?
- Who are its competitors?
- What are their strengths and weaknesses?

If you can answer these questions you should have sufficient background information for the interview. You will be able to relax knowing you can answer any questions about the organisation. Of course, you may not necessarily be asked any direct questions at all but, even if this is the case, you should nevertheless still seek to show the interviewer you've been doing your homework behind the scenes. He may, for example, ask you the question 'What do you do in your spare time?' In reply, you should say something along the lines of:

'Well lately I've been researching your company!..'

He will almost certainly then ask you what you have discovered.

131

Tell him. Similarly, he could ask you the question 'Would you be willing to re-locate if required?' Clearly your answer must be 'Yes', but follow this with a comment to show you've done your research. For example:

'Yes, of course. I'd be pleased to re-locate if it was a step in the right direction. I know you've other plants in Andover and Southampton. I'm sure I'd be happy at either.'

A long list of potential questions is, as previously indicated, given in the following chapter. When you read them through, think how you could draw your homework into each reply.

There are, of course, many ways you can obtain information about an organisation. Study the letter you have received inviting you for an interview. It may well have information which you can use. It may, for example, state who the owners are and where its other outlets are located.

Take another look at the job advertisement which you should have kept. What can you discover from it? Perhaps the organisation indicates the number of people it employs or may comment on its share of the market.

As previously indicated you could also obtain a wealth of company literature from the organisation itself. Most large firms produce promotional literature such as brochures, booklets, catalogues or price lists. If you have not already done so contact the company before the interview for such material. Read and learn.

Why not visit the organisation before the interview? Get the 'feel' of the place. Would you be happy there? See, for example, what products it makes and how they are made. Talk to the staff if you can and hear what they have to say about the organisation's reputation, strengths and weaknesses. Try to pick up a staff magazine or newsletter. What issues are currently of interest or concern?

Find out from the organisation whether 'the trade' has a regularly published magazine or newspaper. For example, the toy trade has a regular monthly magazine called *Toy Trader*. The nursery trade has *Nursery Trader*. Manufacturers, wholesalers and shopkeepers in those trades will read up on current news, views, information and gossip in these magazines. You should too. It will help you to comment in the interview on the organisation, its competitors, their products and the trade in general.

Most trade magazines are published by trade associations. They too will often provide you with helpful information and advice. They will also probably arrange an annual, or bi-annual, trade exhibition where many of the organisations in the trade get together at, perhaps, Earls Court or Olympia in London to show their products and services to other members of the trade and the public. Visit an appropriate trade show if you can. The information you collect on products and competitors will be invaluable in your interview.

If you cannot obtain information on trade magazines, associations or shows from the organisation itself, visit your local library. They should stock a monthly publication called *British Rate and Data* or, as it is commonly known, *BRAD*. This lists the names and publishers of all newspapers and magazines in the United Kingdom.

There will be other books in the library which you can read for reference purposes too. The *Directory of British Associations* will give you the names and addresses of trade associations across the country.

The *Kompass Register* will supply information on many British companies and their products and services.

Dun and Bradstreet's *British Middle Market Directory* and *Guide to Key British Enterprises* will, similarly, give details on many of Britains leading companies. Check them out.

RESEARCHING THE JOB

It is, of course, important that you have an excellent knowledge of the job you have applied for. It is not enough to know you would be a 'trainee manager', a 'clerk' or an 'advertising executive's assistant'. What will you actually do? What will your duties and responsibilities be exactly?

You need to know the answers to these questions because the interviewer may well ask you, 'What makes you think you will be good at this job?' 'What appeals to you most about this job?' or even 'Tell me what you know about this job?' If you want to succeed in the interview you must therefore research the job thoroughly. (See Is this the Job for You? in Chapter One.)

You should, of course, already have obtained a job description and specifications from the company and have kept the job advertisement. Look at these again. Then consider the following:

- What is the job title?
- What exactly does it mean?
- What would be my role and position in the organisation?
- Who would I be answerable to?
- Who would I be responsible for?
- What would I be responsible for?
- What would my principle duties be?
- What are the basic terms and conditions of the job?
- What skills do I need to do the job?
- What qualities do I need to do the job?
- What experience do I need to do the job?

If you can answer these questions, then you should also be able to answer any job related questions you might be asked. Many of the answers to these questions can, as indicated, be found in the job description, specifications or advertisement. Alternatively, you can again approach the organisation and try to talk to an employee in the same or similar capacity. Ask them about the job and what it involves. What difficulties might there be? Think about how you would deal with them. If you're lucky you might even be able to speak to the former holder of the job. What does she or he have to say? Listen and learn from the comments.

You may know someone in another organisation who has a similar job. Talk to them too. Find out anything you can which could be used to your advantage in the interview.

Do remember that in an interview you need to show you've been doing your homework. For example, you could begin your answers to the following questions in the following ways:

'What makes you think you will be good at this job?'
'Well, I've studied your job description and specification carefully and I think I will be good at this job because . . .'

'What appeals to you most about this job?'
'Well, I've been talking to Tony Breadstill who, of course, you've just promoted and he tells me it's a very challenging job. I like a challenge. I'm especially looking forward to . . .'

'Tell me what you know about this job?'
'Well, I've spent the last week researching the job and the company. I've seen, for example, a job description which tells me . . .'

RESEARCHING THE INTERVIEW

You will also want to know about the types of interviews you might face. By far the most common type faced by a school or college leaver is an individual or 'one to one' interview. This should be a fairly relaxed and informal interview between yourself and one interviewer who will often be your direct superior if you get the job. The 'one to one' interview is looked at in more detail in Chapter Seven: The Interview.

Alternatively, you may have to face a panel of interviewers where as many as six different interviewers sit on the opposite side of the table to you. Such interviews are quite common in organisations such as the Civil Service. The panel interview can be fairer than the 'one to one' where the single interviewer's personal bias could creep in.

This type of interview should not provide any unusual or extra difficulties for you and the information given in Chapter Seven is as applicable to panel interviews as it is to individual ones. Just remember that you are dealing with, perhaps, six rather than one interviewer. Pay equal attention and respect to them all. Each one is important.

If there are many applicants, sometimes preliminary interviews are held to cut a long list of 'possibles' to a shorter list of 'probables' who will pass through to a final 'one to one' or 'panel' interview.

Sometimes a preliminary interview will take place on the phone (as explained in Chapter Five: Using the Telephone) This could be quite detailed and cover all the topics and questions indicated in Chapter Seven: The Interview. Alternatively it could concentrate on one key area, such as your past experience.

Sometimes a preliminary, or 'screening' interview will be carried out by an employment agency which is retained by the company. An employee of the agency may meet you in person or talk to you on the telephone and try to match you up with a job specification.

Some organisations will invite you to an informal get-together at a hotel where you may, in the morning, have an informal chat with a junior member of the management. If he or she is impressed you may, in the afternoon, meet the senior recruiting officer for a final, 'one to one' interview.

At the hotel, you may, in the morning, also have to participate in a group interview. The applicants may be asked to get together in a group and discuss a particular topic amongst themselves. The employers watch and assess each group member. Alternatively each applicant may be asked to make an individual speech to the group about, for example, their leisure interests. Again he or she will be assessed.

You can discover beforehand the type of interview you will face by, as always, contacting the organisation. Talk to the personnel department. They should tell you a little about their recruitment procedures, the types of test you might face and even a little about the interviewer. What is he or she like? What interests, hobbies and personal views does he or she have? If you have visited the organisation and can chat informally to other employees, their comments may be illuminating.

You should also read as many books about interviewing as you can. There are many available in your bookshop or library. A list of recommended texts is included in the bibliography at the end of this book.

WIMPY INTERNATIONAL

10 Windmill Road Chiswick London W4 1SD 01 994 6454 Telex 935278 Fax No. 01 995 0563

OUR REF:11ESL017/CAE   1 November 1988

MR M JAMES
13 SHOTLEY ROAD
THRETFORD SURREY
KP17 8NG

Dear Mr James

<u>MANAGEMENT TRAINEE</u>

Thank you for your completed application form in respect of the above position.

After careful consideration I regret to have to inform you that I will not be progressing with your application any further.

I would, however, like to take this opportunity of thanking you for the interest shown by applying for this position and wish you every success for the future.

Yours sincerely

<u>ELLY SLOCOCK</u>
<u>RECRUITMENT OFFICER</u>

A Division of United Biscuits (UK) Ltd. Registered in Scotland, Number 31456 · Registered Office: 12 Hope Street, Edinburgh

WIMPY INTERNATIONAL

10 Windmill Road Chiswick London W4 1SD   01 994 6454 Telex 935278 Fax No. 01 995 0563

OUR REF: 11ESL017/CJF

1 November 1988

MR M JAMES
13 SHOTLEY ROAD
THRETFORD, SURREY
KP17 8NG

Dear Mr JAMES

Thank you for your completed application form for the post of management trainee, I would like to confirm that you are invited to attend an interview at

Wimpy Counter Service
15 Castle Street
Dudley

on Wednesday, 9th November at 2.00 pm.

The interview will be conducted by myself, and any travelling expenses you incur in order to attend the interview will be re-imbursed.

Yours sincerely

ELLY SLOCOCK
RECRUITMENT OFFICER

A Division of United Biscuits (UK) Ltd. Registered in Scotland, Number 31456 · Registered Office: 12 Hope Street, Edinburgh

METROPOLITAN POLICE OFFICE
CADET SELECTION CENTRE PT3(2) BRANCH

PEEL CENTRE
AERODROME ROAD
HENDON, LONDON, NW9

Telephone 01–200 2212 (Switchboard)
01–200 2271 ~~Ox Extn 88~~

BQCA/02

Your ref.:	Our ref.:

Form 8366

Dear

I am writing in connection with your application for a cadetship with the Metropolitan Police Cadet Corps. This has been given careful consdieration and I regret to inform you that you have not been selected for employment.

It is unfortunate that some applicants are not successful, but this situation is inevitable when so many highly qualified candidates are competing for the limited vacancies available.

Your interest in a police career is appreciated and I am sorry to have to disappoint you.

Yours sincerely,

for Recruiting Officer.

METROPOLITAN POLICE OFFICE
CADET SELECTION CENTRE (PT3(2) Branch)

PEEL CENTRE
AERODROME ROAD
HENDON, LONDON, NW9

Telephone 01—200 2212 (Switchboard)
01—200 2272

Your ref. :	Our ref. :

Form 6366

Dear

With reference to your application for appointment within the Metropolitan Police
Cadet Corps, I am pleased to inform you that our initial enquiries have now been
completed and that it is proposed to invite your attendance at our 3 day
residential assessment and selection procedure in due course.

Candidates are normally invited to attend approximately 3-6 months prior to their
18th birthday, with a view to placing those selected on courses commencing on dates
between the ages of 17¾ and 18¼ years. Your attendance will therefore be invited in
                    and a further communication will be sent to you nearer the time.

The selection procedure has been carefully designed to test each candidate's ability
and potential in the area of written and verbal communication (tests include an essay,
group discussion, problem solving and group decision exercises, a lecturette and an
interview) and physical fitness. The physical tests include sprint and endurance
running, bar heaves, a standing long jump and a 100 metres continuous swimming exercise
full details of which are enclosed. Due to the rigorous demands of the course,
candidates must have a very high level of physical fitness in these areas, and you are
advised to take steps to ensure you are able to meet the high standards required.

Yours sincerely,

for Recruiting Officer.

METROPOLITAN POLICE OFFICE
CADET SELECTION CENTRE PT3 (2) BRANCH

PEEL CENTRE
AERODROME ROAD
HENDON, LONDON, NW9

Telephone 01–200 2212 (Switchboard)
           01–200 2272

Your ref.:

Our ref.:

Form 8366

Dear

With reference to your application for appointment as a Metropolitan Police Cadet, I am pleased to invite your attendance at this Centre on Sunday by 8.00pm for our 3 day residential assessment and selection procedure, details of which are contained in the enclosed 'Notes of Guidance' leaflet which you are advised to read carefully. You should take particular note of the items you are required to bring with you (see paragraphs 2.1 and 2.2).

Travelling expenses necessarily incurred in attending will be refunded (second class return rail or bus fares only within the British Isles) on production of your return ticket. Expenses over and above the second class return rail or bus fare must be met by the candidate. All meals and accommodation are provided free of charge. Apart from this, it must be understood that you attend at your own risk and expense. There are no facilities for parking private motor vehicles at the Centre.

Please return the enclosed 'Blue & White' forms to this office (carefully completed in accordance with the instructions thereon) within 10 days, thereby confirming your attendance of the selection procedure. You are also asked to forward two passport size photographs with your name and date of birth written clearly on the back.

If, for any reason, you are unable to attend on the above date, please inform this office immediately.

Please follow the instructions contained in the enclosed 'Notes of Guidance' leaflet carefully, and do not hesitate to contact this office if you require any further information. Emergency contact outside normal office hours can be made through the Duty Officer on 01 200 2243, the Warden on 01 200 2206 or a message can be left on the Centre's answerphone machine (01 200 2100).

Yours sincerely,

for Recruiting Officer.

CHAPTER SEVEN

THE INTERVIEW

FIRST IMPRESSIONS COUNT
- IN THE WAITING ROOM
- YOUR APPEARANCE
- OPENING MOMENTS
- NON VERBAL COMMUNICATION

QUESTIONS AND ANSWERS
- WHAT IS THE INTERVIEWER LOOKING FOR?
- QUESTIONS . . . QUESTIONS . . . QUESTIONS!
- ANSWERS!

THE END OF THE INTERVIEW
- YOUR QUESTIONS
- FOLLOWING THROUGH
- SUCCESS . . . OR FAILURE?

CHAPTER SEVEN

THE INTERVIEW

You must, of course, arrive in good time. The interviewer may be running a tightly scheduled series of twenty minute interviews one after the other. If you're late you'll probably ruin the schedule, and your chances of success. If you're early and the person before you is late, then you can step in and take his place which will be to your benefit. It will make you look good.

FIRST IMPRESSIONS COUNT

In the Waiting Room

Use those last few minutes before your interview for final research. What's the general atmosphere like? Is it formal and deferential or friendly and relaxed? Look and listen to the current employees at work. Are they busy? Do they get on well with each other? Will you fit in? Consider how you were treated when you arrived. Were you warmly welcomed, offered tea and coffee and shown to your seat? Perhaps someone apologised if you were kept waiting. Alternatively, you may have been ignored, had to introduce yourself, find your own seat and sat there in awkward silence. Do you really want to work in such a place?

Try to chat to the receptionist or the secretary. It will help you to relax. In addition you may find out some more useful information about the job, the company or the interviewer. The

145

secretary may also have a close relationship with the interviewer, who may discuss the applicants with her and ask for her opinion. So make a good impression.

If there are other applicants in the room talk to them too. It may help you to loosen up a little. Don't worry if they seem more confident or experienced than you. Appearances can be deceptive.

If there is any company literature lying around take a good look at it. Even if you've seen it before it will help to refresh your memory and, if you haven't, you may pick up some extra points you can use during the interview.

Finally, you should use the time to run through the sort of questions you might be asked and want to ask yourself (refer to 'Questions and Answers'). Make a mental note of any particular points you want to put across. Gather together your thoughts and try to be positive. Remember that the interviewer wouldn't waste time seeing you if he or she didn't think you had the right abilities and skills for the job. If you've got this far you can succeed!

Your Appearance

The interviewer will immediately judge you by the clothes you wear. It's an old, and true, cliché that you should never judge a book by its cover. Unfortunately interviewers often do. It's one of the rules of the game you must abide by if you want to win. It is vitally important that you create the right image.

In general, men should wear a smart, sober suit with a white shirt and a co-ordinated tie. Shoes and socks should be dark, normally black. Women should wear a smart, businesslike dress or, alternatively, a blouse and skirt beneath a matching jacket. Wear low heels.

If you can afford to buy a new shirt or blouse, it will help you to feel fresh and confident and will also indicate to the interviewer that you've made a special effort. Alternatively, keep your 'best' clothes just for interviews if you can. Always make sure they are clean and tidy. Brush jackets, check buttons, press trousers, shirts and blouses and polish shoes. Do make sure that they are also comfortable. Don't try to squeeze into a pair of tight trousers because you think they'll make you look slimmer. You'll then sit there feeling hot and edgy. Be sensible. Avoid clothes that are tight, itchy, excessively fashionable or too thick or thin for the time of year.

Have your hair cut several days before the interview. If you have it cut too close to the interview it may make you feel on edge. Make sure your hair is acceptable. Outrageous styles, lengths and colours may impress your friends but will rarely impress an interviewer and potential employer. Remember to shave before the interview. Few employers are impressed by designer stubble. Shave the night before if it will help you to feel more comfortable at the interview. Trim and tidy your moustache or beard if you have one.

You must also pay careful attention to the sensitive area of personal hygiene. BO is unpleasant and a sign of laziness and bad manners. No-one wants to employ or work with a person with BO. Have a bath or shower before the interview and wash your hair too. Use a mouth wash, spray or suck a strong mint if you think you might have bad breath. It will also disguise the fact that you may have been drinking or smoking; both of which, incidentally, are most inadvisable before an interview. Drinking will dull your senses when you should be at your best and smoking may be viewed as unpleasant by many employers.

Carry a small vanity mirror in your top pocket or handbag and check your face before entering the interview room. If you've just eaten lunch (often inadvisable in case you drop food down your front) you may have food in your teeth or crumbs in your beard. Be careful!

Opening Moments

You may be met by the interviewer in person, guided to the room by a secretary or have to find the room yourself (all of which will help you to judge if this is the type of firm you want to work for). Remember to leave your overcoat or bags at the desk. If, for example, you entered the interview room carrying your coat, handbag, briefcase and two bags of shopping (as some applicants do) it looks very unprofessional indeed. It can also be embarrassing when you have to shake hands. So, be businesslike. Unload excess baggage.

Whether you're met by the interviewer in the reception area or you meet him or her in the interview room, the 'rules' are the same. Meet him with a warm smile and, however nervous you are, look him in the eye and greet him: 'Hallo' . . . 'Good Morning..' etc. If you've done your research you'll know his or her name. Use it, he may be impressed especially if he didn't think you'd know. Try to speak first as it indicates confidence and, in addition, be prepared to make 'ice breaking' small talk. 'Good afternoon, Mr Reynolds, I'm pleased to meet you' could be your opening comment, but try to follow this with a few words which will spark a pleasant conversation. It will, of course, depend on the situation. If you meet in the office then a picture on the wall, the view from the window or something unusual on the desk may catch your eye.

If he met you in the corridor or reception area you could thank him and, if humour seems appropriate, joke that you were worried you would otherwise have found your way into the broom cupboard! Be very careful about using humour though. As with all interviews, play it by ear. It depends on what the interviewer is like – and only you can be the judge.

When you enter the interview room do not sit until you are invited to do so and do not sit in the interviewer's seat as sometimes happens. Wait until he indicates which seat you should sit in. You may be offered a cup of tea or coffee. Do not accept. If you're trying to drink and answer questions something will often go wrong. You'll either slurp, choke, be distracted or be expected to answer at the exact moment you're drinking. You may irritate the interviewer by fiddling with the cup, saucer or spoon. If you're very nervous you may even spill it. So it's better to be safe than sorry and graciously refuse, 'Thank you, but no, I've just had one'. For similar reasons also politely refuse an offer of a cigarette or sweets. The chances are you won't make an embarrassing gaffe but it does sometimes happen, so don't take the risk.

'Non-verbal Communication'

You're doing well. You're punctual, the interviewer likes your appearance and you've made pleasant small talk. Many interviewers make decisions about applicants within those first few minutes. As such, you must be a winner. There is, however, still some way to go and you must convince him that the initial, favourable impression was correct.

One factor that will help is, perhaps surprisingly, your 'non-verbal communication'! It's not just what you say, it's how you say it. What 'hidden messages' do you transmit?

As indicated, you should have regular eye contact with the interviewer. Look at him with a steady gaze when he asks you a question. It shows you are listening. Look at him regularly as you reply. An interviewer will not be impressed with an applicant who looks at the floor, ceiling or out of the window. He will assume, often correctly, that the applicant is either shifty or not really interested. Test the theory. Ask a friend or colleague to play the part of such an applicant whilst you ask him questions. You'll find it a rude and annoying habit.

When you speak, make sure your voice is clear and steady. Try not to gabble, roll or slur your words. Make sure the interviewer can understand what you're saying. Don't speak too slowly though. He'll think you're either a little backward or patronising him. Don't speak in a dull monotone either. Show vigour, enthusiasm and interest in your voice. (See 'Using Your Voice Effectively' in Chapter Five, page 117.)

Keep your body still, calm and relaxed. Don't fidget or tap your feet. Don't bite your lip or your nails (which would, also, incidentally, obscure your voice). Don't fiddle with buttons or rings. You want to create the impression that you are confident and in control. If you are hunched up in your seat, gripping the sides with clenched fists then it will be obvious that you are not . . . and who's going to employ someone that nervous?

At the same time, don't sprawl back with arms and legs spread far and wide. You'll look overconfident . . . and who's going to employ someone who appears to be an arrogant bighead?

As a general rule lean slightly forward which indicates interest and attentiveness. Hold your hands in your lap. Don't wave them about or gesticulate wildly which is annoying, and don't fold your arms across your chest which always looks ill mannered. Tuck your legs in together close to your seat. Keep your seat, incidentally, at a reasonable distance from the interviewer's desk. Some applicants when offered a chair move it as close to the desk as possible and during the interview even lean on the desk. They think it indicates friendliness. It doesn't. It is rude and disrespectful. Don't do it.

QUESTIONS AND ANSWERS

What is the interviewer looking for?

As I have said throughout the book, the potential employer is not simply looking for the applicant with the most qualifications, experience or the best personality. To obtain a job you must offer a range of qualities. No text can state exactly what is required because, of course, every employer is different and so their values and methods of assessment will all vary. To have got to the interview stage you will, in your application form, letter, C.V. or telephone call have shown that you have the basic qualities the employer is looking for. Now that you are sitting in front of the interviewer he or she will be trying to assess you further in a number of areas. For example, he may be asking himself if you are:

A Team Member The employer will need to consider how you will fit into the current team. Will you get on with your superiors, colleagues and subordinates? Can you communicate well? Alternatively, will you be disruptive and disagreeable?

Mature The employer will need to consider whether you will be a mature and responsible employee. He will consider your appearance, speech, manners and behaviour. Do you, for example, respond well to criticism or do you try to shift the blame onto others? Are you serious and sensible? How confident are you? You should be well balanced and aware of your own abilities without being arrogant, pompous or overbearing. You should be positive, on the ball, open and friendly. A warm smile and a touch of humour won't go amiss. You must be reliable, honest and hardworking. Will you turn up for work on time, work to the best of your ability and take pride in your efforts? Can you weigh up facts and make balanced decisions?

Motivated Every employee should be motivated. He or she should have drive and ambition and should want to succeed at every task. An employer will be looking for employees who can be promoted. You should be energetic, accept a challenge and always strive to do that little bit more. You should also show initiative and be able to make decisions on your own.

Knowledgable Do you have the education and training to allow you to actually do the job properly? Do you have enough practical experience to handle the work? Are you intelligent enough? Are you quick to learn and understand information? Can you keep up with changes and new developments?

As indicated, each interviewer will consider each area to be of varying importance. Try to judge (depending on the job you've applied for) how your interviewer will grade each area and bear that in mind during the interview. For example, being a good team member is most important if it is a job where results are achieved through group efforts. So plug away at your 'team spirit' and refer to your past experience to support this. For example, 'I was in the college rugby and cricket team.' Alternatively, if you were applying for a job where you worked largely alone, then other qualities such as motivation should be stressed. For example, prove (from your past work) how you have been self-motivated to meet deadlines and schedules.

The interviewer will look for the appropriate qualities in you by asking a series of questions and listening carefully to your answers. Don't worry if you see him making notes during your interview. He will probably be jotting down points about you which, of course, he needs to do if he's interviewing dozens of applicants. He may also have a marking system divided into the areas indicated. Then, at the end of all the interviews, he can easily compare applicants with each other. Look at the marking systems on the following pages. They will help you to assess how different organisations judge their applicants. Think how highly you would score in each particular area.

Questions . . . Questions . . . Questions!

The list of questions you could be asked is potentially endless. It depends on the interviewer. Similarly you can never predict the length of the interview or its order. Every interview is different. Some texts describe how a 'typical' interview will develop, will give you 'typical' examples of an interview 'in action' and will even give you a long list of endless questions and tell you how you should reply to each and every one.

You cannot learn in this way. No question will be asked in exactly the way you imagined. In the spotlight you will never remember your rehearsed reply; and even if you did, wouldn't it sound stilted? To succeed in an interview all you can do is think generally about the sort of questions you could be asked and loosely think about the sort of reply you would give. The important thing is that you have the confidence to answer every question by thinking on your feet. You must be on the ball.

To ascertain whether you have the qualities listed on the organisation's particular marking system, the interviewer will ask you a number of questions which, for your convenience, could be unofficially grouped into three main areas.

Personal Questions

These questions could, perhaps, be further divided up into four categories. Read them through to make sure you would feel confident of your replies. You should also try to think why particular questions are asked. What specific quality is the interviewer trying to find in you?

Family Background : What do your parents do for a living?
                      : Do you have any brothers or sisters?

:How do your parents feel about this job?

These types of question (and I'm sure you can think of many more) may be used to get you talking as you will obviously find it easy to talk about yourself. If you're young and still live at home then it's also of some relevance. For example, if your father was a salesman who was transferred regularly then he may have to move home again shortly. How would that affect you? Questions about your family background can also serve to show how motivated you are. If you came from, perhaps, a disadvantaged background and had succeeded against the odds then you would, of course, be viewed favourably. 'Family background' questions help to create a fuller picture of you beyond the basic details on your C.V. or application form. Don't resent them or consider them intrusive. Be open and friendly. Always talk with interest about your family even if you dislike them. You should appear mature and well balanced.

Personal Characteristics

- What sort of person are you?
- Describe your personality.
- What's your best feature?
- What's your worst feature?
- Can you cope with pressure?
- Tell me a little about yourself.
- Describe yourself as others see you.
- Do you have many friends?
- Are you popular?
- What makes you tick?
- What's your motivation?
- What's special about you?

Often, these questions are asked to see how mature you are. Can you see yourself as others see you? Can you judge your strengths and weaknesses? The interviewer may ask you about your friends to see the type of people you mix with. He could even ask you who your 'heroes' are and why you admire them to judge what sort of values you have and what qualities you

153

admire. He also wants to see what drives you on and motivates you: money, a challenge, recognition?

When you answer these questions it is important to show that you are mature. Show modesty when you talk of your successes. Saying, for example, that others were a great help in your achievements will indicate maturity and that you recognise other people's knowledge and experience. If you're asked to indicate your weaknesses ('What's your worst feature?' 'Tell me a little about yourself' or 'Describe yourself as others see you') you should never, of course, say anything such as 'I have no weaknesses' even if you say it with humour. Everyone has faults or weaknesses and a mature person recognises them. You should admit to a weakness but, at the same time, don't be too honest. 'I lose my temper easily', 'I can't get up in the morning' or similar comments should never be made. Try to make your weakness sound like a strength. For example:

> 'I suppose my weakness is that I always want to see the job through to the very end.' (which makes it sound remarkably like a strength)

or

> 'I suppose my weakness is that I'm too much of a perfectionist.' (again this is made to sound like a strength). 'I always want to do the job just right.'

If you're asked about your friends try to suggest they are very close to what you think the interviewer would perceive as an ideal employee. Similarly, choose 'sensible' heroes who have qualities that the interviewer would perceive as good.

If you talk about motivation you should avoid comments about money. You're looking for 'a challenge', 'a chance to get on in life' or 'to improve and stretch myself'. Think about your answers to these example questions:

Leisure Interests

- What do you do in your spare time?
- Why do you enjoy that?

- Do you play sport at all?
- What type of sport do you like?
- Do you read at all?
- What sort of books do you read?
- What's your daily paper?
- Are you competitive?
- Would you say you're a team player or an individual?
- Do you belong to any clubs or societies?

You will often be asked about your leisure interests so the employer can gain a fuller picture of you. He wants to know that you believe life exists outside of school and have outside interests, which is a healthy sign. He'll also want to find out if you're a team member or an individualist. Style your replies according to the job you have applied for.

Health

- Are you fit?
- This job is very tiring. Are you up to it physically and mentally?
- Are you used to pressure?
- Have you ever had any health problems?

Questions about your health will probably not be raised unless you've indicated a problem on your application form or if the job can be particularly tiring. You may, for example, be involved in constant heavy lifting and the interviewer will want to know you're up to the job. Similarly you may be applying for a job as a travelling salesman which involves regular driving.

Think about the particular job you have applied for and, if you feel questions are likely, be prepared to answer and substantiate your answers. For example, if you were applying for a stockroom job, you'd probably be asked a question such as 'Can you handle regular loading and unloading of heavy goods?' You could reply, 'Yes. I work out with weights twice a week at the local sports club so I'm sure I can handle the work.'

Education

Clearly, if you've just left school, college or university then you must expect much of the interview to be based around your education. Think how you'd answer these questions. Why do you think each one is asked?

- Why did you do these subjects?
- Which was your favourite subject?
- Why was it your favourite subject?
- Which subject did you most dislike?
- Why didn't you like it?
- What was your best subject?
- What was your worst subject?
- Would you do the same subjects if you could choose again?
- How well do you think you did?
- Could you have done better?
- Do you think your results were fair?
- Do you think exams are important?
- Did you do anything special at school?
- What did you do in your free time?
- Did you like games?
- What about teams? Did you play for any?
- Did you belong to any clubs or societies?
- What were your teachers like?
- Did you get on well with your teachers?
- Did you like your school?
- What did you like most about school?
- What did you like least about school?

Obviously some questions are designed to check facts. Others such as 'How well do you think you did?' and 'Could you have done better?' are designed to see how balanced and mature you are and how you assess facts and reach rational decisions. Do you blame others for poor results (bad teachers, a particularly difficult exam or bad markers) or do you accept that, perhaps, you could have worked a little harder in one or two subjects? Never seek to shift the blame. You should accept responsibility. For example, 'I didn't do very well because I had some dreadful teachers who didn't know what they were talking about' may, perhaps, be true but you shouldn't say it. You could say, 'I didn't do quite as well as expected in some subjects. To be honest I worked harder in my favourite subjects than the others which, looking back, was a mistake.' This would be a better response. There is nothing wrong with admitting to a mistake (everyone makes them) as long as you show you learned from it.

Experience

If you've worked before, then the interviewer will probably concentrate on your work experience rather than your education. It does, of course, depend on the interviewer. Questions can very loosely be divided into two groups.

Questions about your current or past jobs:

- Tell me about your work experience.
- How well do you think you've done so far in your career?
- What did you learn from each job?
- Why were you unemployed for such a long time?
- Why did you change jobs so often?
- How exactly did you get your last job?
- What exactly did you do in your last job?
- Give me an idea of what you did in a typical day.
- How did you get on with your colleagues?
- Did you get on well with your last boss?
- Did you like your boss?
- Did you ever fall out with him/her?
- What did you like most about the job?
- What did you dislike most about the job?
- How good are you at your job?
- What did you do best?
- What did you do badly?
- Did you ever make mistakes?
- What sort of decisions did you have to make?
- Why did you leave?
- You weren't sacked, were you?

Questions about this job you are applying for:

- Why do you want this job?
- What do you know about this job?
- What's the most interesting aspect of the job?

- What's the most boring aspect of the job?
- What do you know about this company?
- Do you know who the owner is?
- Would you be willing to move about if we asked you to?
- Would you be willing to work overtime?
- Can you work irregular hours/evenings/weekends if we asked you to?
- Are you experienced enough for this job?
- Where do you see yourself in five years time?
- How do you see yourself progressing?
- How much money do you want?
- What will you do if you fail to get this job?
- What would you say if I said I don't think you're right for this job?
- Why should I give you this job?

Again, you should think for yourself why exactly each question is asked. What's the interviewer looking for? How should you answer each question? Run through them until you're happy with your own particular response. What would the 'ideal' employee say?

ANSWERS!

You now need to know a little more about how to answer the interviewer's questions to show you've got the desired qualities. As stated, you cannot plan an exact answer to every possible question, but you should know how to respond generally. There are a number of different styles of questions which require different responses. Read through the following sections which are also full of examples from the sample questions given. Once you have read them all return to the 'Questions . . .' section, re-read it and think about your replies again until you're absolutely confident of them.

Closed Questions

Many questions can, theoretically, be described as 'closed'. These questions require a simple yes or no answer. For example:

- Did you like your school?
- Were you good at mathematics?
- Did you get on well with your last boss?

These types of questions are often asked by an inexperienced or incompetent interviewer. Clearly a yes/no answer is going to reveal very little about the applicant. To be fair though such questions do have their place. They can be used to confirm facts. 'I see you have a number of CSE's. Do you have the equivalent of four 'O' levels?' and, if the applicant clams up, an experienced interviewer may use them just to keep the conversation moving.

If you are asked a closed question then give a straight yes or no answer but try to expand it a little. For example, in response to the first example you might say something along the lines of:

'Yes, I enjoyed school very much. I hope this shows in my exam results and my other activities there.'

Such a response shows you have the confidence to make conversation. It also gives you the chance to take the questioning into areas which you can talk about further and which are flattering to you. Your excellent exam results show you are hardworking and intelligent. Your other activities (playing for the school football and cricket teams) show you have healthy outside interests and are a good 'team member'.

Your reply to the second question could be:

'Yes. I was quite . . . (be modest) . . . good at maths. As you can see I obtained a grade 'B' and sat the exam a year early.'

or:

'No . . . I found the subject difficult . . . (this shows honesty) . . .

I'm planning to re-sit the exam at night school as it will help me with my work.' (This shows you are hardworking and ambitious.)

Remember: always expand a little. Keep trying to score points. However, do avoid rambling on. Don't be a bore. Say what you have to say quickly and then shut up.

The third question, 'Did you get on well with your last boss', leads onto the second group of questions.

Leading Questions

There are some questions where the 'right' answer is clearly signposted.

For example, 'Did you get on well with your last boss?' is, if you like, still a closed yes/no question, but the answer you should give is obvious. You should therefore say something like:

'Yes, we got on well. I learned a great deal from her. She was a good manager.' (This shows you get on well with people and can learn from them.)

Other leading questions could include:

'Can you cope with pressure?'
'Are you experienced enough for this job?'

Clearly both answers must be 'Yes.' Again elaborate a little and try to support your answers with facts.

'Yes . . . at my last job I worked to a very tight schedule. I am used to producing good work to a deadline.'
'Yes . . . I admit I have never actually run a department before but I've experience of leadership from my university days. As you'll see from the C.V. I was secretary of the student union. In addition I stood in for my last boss during her holiday.' (Always substantiate your response and expand with facts.)

Limited Questions

There are some questions where your reply will be limited. For example:

'Who was your boss at Barham and Brown?'
'When did you pass your 'O' levels?'
'Where did you sit your 'A' levels?'

Clearly, these questions can allow a short answer but, as always, try to expand a little. You want to have a conversation rather than a cold question and answer session.

These questions could be answered:

'I worked for Mrs (this shows respect) Barham, the original owner. I learned a great deal from her.' It goes without saying that you do not criticise former employers or colleagues. Bitterness, anger, hatred or contempt are not admirable. Always have a good word to say about them whatever you really feel.

'I passed them in June 1984' – Such an answer could be a satisfactory response to the second question but, of course, this information should already be on the C.V. or application form. If it is not, you should add, 'I'm sorry I forgot to make a note of that for you'.

You can, of course, make mistakes. Don't be afraid to admit to them and say you're sorry. If you did make a note on the C.V. you could say:

'I passed them in June 1984. Did I forget to put that in my C.V.?' Remember you don't want to make the interviewer look foolish by pointing it out directly. Show some discretion.

'Where did you sit your 'A' levels?' may, perhaps, be answered in a similar fashion or 'I sat them at Thretford Secondary School. I was fortunate enough to have some excellent teachers there and they helped me get the results I did.' Again, it does no harm to praise your 'bosses' and it helps to show a little modesty too. Maybe you got three 'B's' but don't boast about them.

Open Questions

Some questions (How, why, what?) allow you to give open ended answers. For example:

'How well do you think you've done so far in your career?'
'How good are you at your job?'
'Why should I give you this job?'
'What are your best qualities?'
'What are your worst features?'

If you are well prepared, have thought about the type of question you may be asked and know the points you want to raise, then these questions are absolute gifts. It's your chance to start putting across those points. Assemble your thoughts and mentally jot down the points you're going to make. It's important that you make them in a clear and logical manner. Be direct. Don't drone on. Use bright, lively words in an enthusiastic voice. Support your statements with examples and facts.

Effectively, you're being invited to sell yourself. Go for it but do remember not to be too boastful. Be modest.

For example, in response to the first question you could say something along the lines of:

'I'm quite pleased at my progress so far . . . (if you're not you don't want to admit it, if you are then you want to appear modest) . . . I've had three jobs as you know and each time I've taken a step upwards – promotion, if you like. I've enjoyed each job, got on well with everybody and learnt something from each. I'm improving all the time and feel I'm contributing more to each company as I improve.'

As you can see several good points have been put across. Of course, there is no right or wrong answer. Think about yours. How would you answer this and the other questions?

Hypothetical Questions

Sometimes you'll be asked a question which starts 'What would you do if . . .' Clearly it's hypothetical so often you won't really know what you'd do. Don't tell the interviewer that though, that's not the answer he's looking for. Try to think what sort of employee he wants. Then imagine you are that ideal employee. What would the ideal employee do?

Multiple Questions

Some incompetent interviewers may ask you several questions at the same time. For example

> 'You read books then? What sort do you like? Have you ever read any of JACK SHARP's? He usually writes about our sort of business, doesn't he?'

or:

> 'I see from your application form that you play rugby. What team do you play for? Is it in a league or do you play for fun?'

However bad the interviewer is you must remember not to interrupt, patronise or condescend. If you jump in before he's finished speaking it looks bad and if you said (as some do), 'I've told you that already' or 'It's on the form, isn't it?' then you might as well leave now. Listen and look. Wait until he's finished (he may look at you, smile, nod or pause) and then answer. Be simple and direct. Such convoluted questions can, if you think about them, give you the opportunity to give a well structured reply. You can also, if you're clever, turn the question back to him to keep the conversation moving.

For example:

> 'Yes, I do read books and I do like JACK SHARP's work. As a matter of fact it was his books that got me interested in this type of business. What do you think of him?'

or:

> '. . . To be honest I haven't read any of his work but I'd be very interested to. Can you tell me the titles?'

163

Similarly:

'I play for the Thretford Old Boys' team. We play in the Old Boys Sunday League. It's great fun. Do you play rugby?'

Unexpected Questions

Finally, and of great importance, there are those unexpected questions that crop up every so often. No matter how many texts you read and how many questions you think might be asked, there will always be one or two which throw you. They may be under the subjects already discussed. They may perhaps be the same question as ones you've prepared to answer but be asked in a different way.

For example, you may prepare for the question 'Why did you leave?' and in previous chapters we've discussed 'good' and 'bad' reasons. You may even have prepared a little speech. Then the interviewer asks 'You weren't sacked, were you?' which could throw you completely. If you think about it you can keep calm and give largely the same answer. If you have been sacked and were planning to disguise it then the interviewer may have thrown you off balance. Don't panic. Listen and assess.

There may be questions about the interviewer's pet subjects. I have heard such questions as:

'What do you think of the way Chelsea just dumped their manager?'

'What do you think of this Scargill bloke then?'

A response can be difficult. The questions come out of the blue, you've nothing prepared and often you'll know nothing about the subject. Sometimes you may be able to guess what the 'right' answer would be the way the question is phrased. If you look at the questions again you could see that 'just dumped' in the first indicated the interviewer 'supported' the manager rather than the club and 'this Scargill bloke' instead of 'Arthur Scargill' indicates his feelings in the second. Listen carefully and answer accordingly.

If no indication is given try, if possible, to make a fairly neutral comment observing both sides of the argument without coming to any conclusion. You could always conclude with 'What's your opinion, Mr Reynolds?'

Of course you may not have an answer or know anything about the subject so be honest. For example, 'I'm very sorry but I really don't know anything about that. Could you tell me a little bit about it?' (which shows you are interested to learn).

Such questions (and they do crop up) can cause your mind to go blank. The question is so obscure that you can't think of anything. Don't worry, it happens all the time. Tell the interviewer, 'I'm very sorry but my mind's gone blank. Could we move on and return to that later?' With luck, you'll then have time to gather your thoughts.

THE END OF THE INTERVIEW

Your Questions

Towards the end of the interview you will normally be given the opportunity to ask questions. These may, in fact, have been answered already. The interviewer may have talked about the company or job in an opening speech and commented on the various points during the interview. Nevertheless you should still try to raise two or three questions if you can. It shows you're still enthusiastic and interested. Don't, however, ask too many (there are other applicants). Do try to raise valid questions. 'What time is the next bus?' or 'Where's the nearest railway station?' (and both questions have been asked) will not win you any points.

Consider questions around the following areas:

Colleagues If the points have not been raised you could ask who your immediate superiors and subordinates would be. But do make sure before you ask the question that the interviewer isn't your immediate superior, otherwise you'll look foolish because you should really have known that. You could also ask what happened to the last occupant of the job. If he or she was promoted then, of course, that's good. You can mention that you'd look forward to meeting him or her to discuss the job which shows initiative on your part. If he's left the company, find out why.

Responsibilities Are there any special problems you might face and should know about? You may be running a brand new department, working with new suppliers or inexperienced staff. You need to know. If there are any problems indicated, try to say how you'd deal with them which again shows initiative.

Your Future Employers want an employee who is a good investment. They look to the future and may have you in mind for future promotion. You want, if you have not already done so, to indicate that you are ambitious (but, of course, not *too* ambitious). You could ask questions along the lines of, 'If you were to offer me the job..(never assume you've got it however well you've done)..how would you see my future with you?' or 'I am very keen to join such a successful company..(a little enthusiasm and flattery never go amiss)..and would like to know a little more about future prospects.'

Training If this is your first job you may want to know a little more about the training they offer. They may, as some companies do, allow you paid time off to attend college on a day release basis and also pay for books and exam fees. Why not say, 'I am very keen to continue my education which would help me in this job. Do you have any training facilities to assist me?'

Money, Terms and Conditions It is, of course, vitally important that you know what your salary is. It may already have been covered as might other important details such as holidays, pensions and fringe benefits. If not you should ask. You may at the very end be offered the job on the spot. It's unlikely, of course, but it does sometimes happen if you're the last candidate interviewed. If so you will need to know the exact terms and conditions before you accept. Otherwise you might hand in your notice, start work for the new company and find out you're not getting exactly what you expected. If in doubt ask towards the end of the interview. Make it your last question and, to show that you're not concerned simply with this aspect of the job, start your question along the lines of, 'I don't want you to think I'm solely concerned with money, but I wonder if you could just confirm the exact salary/holiday allowance.'

If you have no questions, you'll have to say something like: 'Thank you. I did have a number of questions to ask but you've been good enough to deal with my points during the interview.'

At the end of the interview try to behave in the same way as you did when you entered. Remain relaxed even if you feel more inclined to escape as quickly as you can. Shake hands, smile and thank the interviewer for interviewing you. If he hasn't indicated when he'll be in touch then you should ask. It is not an unreasonable question as you, presumably, have other possible job offers in the pipeline. (Don't tell him that though as it looks as though you're trying to rush him.) Simply say, 'I hope you don't mind me asking but could you tell me when you'll be making your decision?' He should tell you.

FOLLOWING THROUGH

The interview is over and, by and large, you'll probably know if you're in with a chance or not. Whatever you think you must follow up the interview by writing to the interviewer. It is very important. The reason for this is to try to keep one step ahead of the other applicants, make you stand out from the crowd and keep you in the employer's mind.

Your letter should contain the following points.

- Thank the interviewer for the interview.
- Raise any points you failed to mention in the interview.
- Include any items you promised to send on (photocopies of certificates, details of referees etc).

167

- Re-confirm your interest in the job and say that if it is offered, you would be pleased to accept.

If you're in with a chance of the job such a letter could tip the balance in your favour. Even if you are not, it is still courteous to send one and, you never know, the employer may be impressed enough to change his mind, offer you a different job or keep your details on file for future reference. It does happen. Send the letter by first class post on the same day as the interview or, at the latest, the day after.

Never harass the interviewer by telephoning, calling personally or writing again if he takes time to reach a decision. It makes you look desperate. It will not create a favourable impression.

SUCCESS . . . OR FAILURE?

If all goes well, you will receive a written offer of employment. Examples are given on pages 171–173. You should not, even at this stage, stop job hunting or hand in your notice though. The offer will usually be subject to references (refer to the section on References in Chapter Two) and possibly a medical report. In addition you will need to be sure of all the terms and conditions of a job before you accept. If you have any doubts then you must check. At this stage they will not be offended if you ask searching questions about, for example, overtime, training or holidays.

Once your references, the medical report and your questions have all been dealt with, then you can hand in your notice. Resign graciously. Act in a mature fashion. Always be nice to people on the way up. You may one day pass them again on the way down.

You should also, of course, write to your new employer to accept the job offer. For example;

Dear Mr Reynolds

re: TRAINEE MANAGER
Thank you for your letter of 12 September offering me the above
position subject to satisfactory references.

I am pleased to confirm that the terms and conditions – as
detailed in your letter and our subsequent conversation – are
acceptable. As such, I am delighted to accept your offer. I can
confirm that I can start work on Monday 25 September at nine
o'clock.

I look forward to meeting you again and working for your
excellent company.

Yours sincerely

Michael James

M James

Of course, you may fail. Sometimes you will receive a rejection
letter. Examples of rejection letters are given on pages 137, 139
and 174. Don't just screw them up and throw them in the waste
paper basket. Read them. You may find that the interviewer
has actually taken the time to write a personal, rather than a
standard, company reply. Learn from it. He or she may indicate
why you did not get the job. If they do not it can still be worth
contacting them to see if they will tell you. After all, they've
taken the time and trouble to write so, if you're polite, calm
and friendly, they may spare you a few minutes on the phone.
If the rejection letter, and subsequent conversation, were amic-
able you might also consider asking the firm to keep your name
on file for future reference. Another vacancy may arise in the
future.

Some companies, it must be said, do not reply. Unfortunately
these, nowadays, seem to be in the majority. Please do not take
it as a personal slur. It is simply that they are extremely rude
and ill-mannered. I doubt that you would enjoy working for
such companies.

If you do fail to get a particular job, don't worry. It happens
to everyone. Most jobhunters become used to the taste of rejection. Try, however, to learn from it. Why did you 'fail'? Think

about the interview, the questions, and the interviewer. Where exactly did you go wrong and how can you improve for next time? Often it's a case of practice makes perfect. One day you will succeed. Good luck and good hunting!

If, of course, you are a successful job hunter you may receive several offers. If so, do think carefully about your long-term ambition. Accept the job which will give you the best opportunity to achieve that ambition. Choose the job which is a step in the right direction.

You must then immediately write and politely turn down any other job offer. This is important. One day you may want to approach that employer again. For example:

Dear Mr Reynolds

re: TRAINEE MANAGER
Many thanks for your letter of 12 September offering me the above position subject to references.

However, I have been fortunate to receive several excellent opportunities at the same time. After very careful consideration I have decided to accept another offer and, as such, felt I must immediately write to inform you of this difficult decision.

Thank you nevertheless for your offer which I was flattered to receive.

Yours sincerely

Michael James

M James

Imperial Chemical House
Millbank London SW1P 3JF

Telephone 01-834 4444
Telex 21324

SLTR-1/DOC2
MONTHLY STAFF - INFORMAL OFFER LETTER

_____
_____
_____
_____
_____

Your ref	Our ref	Tel ext	Date
_____	_____	_____	_____

Dear _____

Thank you for coming to Millbank for interview in connection with
our vacancy for _____.

I am very pleased to be able to offer you this position at a
starting salary of £_____ per annum, plus a London Allowance of
£_____. The job is at present Grade _____.

As you know, this offer is subject to our receiving a satisfactory
medical report and references and I hope it will be convenient for
you to come here on _____ at _____ for an
examination. Please come to Reception and ask to be directed to our
Medical Department.

I should be glad if you would let me know in writing if you wish to
accept this offer and the date on which you would be free to start.

Yours sincerely

_____
Personnel Officer
Head Office Personnel Section

WIMPY INTERNATIONAL

10 Windmill Road Chiswick London W4 1SD   01 994 6454 Telex 935278 Fax No. 01 995 0563

OUR REF:11ESL017/CAE   1 November 1988

MR M JAMES
13 SHOTLEY ROAD
THRETFORD, SURREY
KP17 8NG

Dear MIKE,

I am pleased to offer you a position as Management Trainee in the Counter
Service Division of Wimpy International starting on Monday, 7 November 1988.
There will be a minimum of 12 weeks initial training and, subject to your
performance, you will be appointed Duty Manager at the end of the training.
Your progress beyond all that will be subject to your capabilities.

Your starting salary will be £8,250 plus £730 in respect of London Weighting
per annum and payable monthly, in arrears, to your bank. You will be entitled
to free meals during working hours. There are no set hours of work as these
will depend on the nature of the business; you will also be required to work
shifts, weekends and statutory holidays.

This appointment is subject to the receipt of satisfactory references and a
satisfactory medical report.

Your training will take place in our Gloucester Road Restaurant.

I trust that you find the terms of this offer acceptable, please fill out the
attached forms and return them to me. It is important that you do this as
soon as possible to ensure that satisfactory arrangements for your
accommodation and training can be made. Please report to the above offices on
your first day at 12 noon, bringing with you your bank details and National
Insurance number.

Yours sincerely

ELLY SLOCOCK
RECRUITMENT OFFICER

Encs

UB A Division of United Biscuits (UK) Ltd. Registered in Scotland, Number 31456 · Registered Office: 12 Hope Street, Edinburgh

METROPOLITAN POLICE OFFICE
CADET SELECTION CENTRE PT3(2) BRANCH

PEEL CENTRE
AERODROME ROAD
HENDON, LONDON, NW9

Telephone 01—200 2212 (Switchboard)
01—200 2272

Your ref. :	Our ref. :

Form 6366

Dear

You have been successful in your application to join the Metropolitan Police
Cadet Corps and the Commissioner is pleased to offer you a vacancy. To take
up this offer you are requested to report to the above address not later than
5pm on Sunday   prior to commencing training on the following
day. Contact telephone number for urgent queries <u>on that day only</u> is 01-200 2206.

Will you please complete and return the enclosed schedule of employment, in
the envelope provided, <u>as soon as possible.</u>

If you obtain further employment before joining the Cadet Corps, or you become
employed, please notify this office immediately giving full details. You should
nominate a responsible person other than a relative, who can certify that you
were unemployed at any period, and who can testify as to your character during
that time.

You are reminded that you must inform this office immediately of <u>any</u> injury or
illness or adverse contact with police, and that failure to do so will almost
certainly result in your entry to the Metropolitan Police Cadet Corps being
deferred or possibly the offer of appointment being withdrawn.

Although you will normally be free from 5.15 pm on Fridays, during some weekends
you will be required to take part in sporting and other activities. Leave will
be taken at fixed periods. Other leave will only be granted in special
circumstances on compassionate grounds at the discretion of the Commissioner.

There are no parking facilities for cars, motorcycles or mopeds at the Cadet
School, neither is there parking in the immediate vicinity of Hendon and street
parking is very limited.

Please note that this offer of employment is made on the distinct understanding
that your character references and suitability remain satisfactory to the
Commissioner who reserves the right to rescind this offer up to the actual time
of joining the Cadet Corps, or to terminate the cadetship should your response
to training not be up to the required standard.

Please read carefully the enclosed correspondence.

Yours sincerely,

for Recruiting Officer.

173

Imperial Chemical House
Millbank London SW1P 3JF

Telephone 01-834 4444
Telex 21324

Imperial
Chemical
Industries
PLC

SLTR-3/DOC9
EXTERNAL - TURN DOWN AFTER INTERVIEW

_____
_____
_____
_____
_____

Your ref   Our ref   Tel ext   Date

_____   _____   _____   _____

Dear _____

Thank you for attending for interview in connection with our vacancy
for _____.

We have now been able to give your application careful consideration
but regret to say we feel unable to offer you this position.

I am sorry if this is a disappointment but hope you are soon
successful in finding a suitable post elsewhere.

Yours sincerely

_____
Personnel Officer
Head Office Personnel Section

Imperial Chemical House
Millbank London SW1P 3JF

Telephone 01-834 4444
Telex 21324

Imperial
Chemical
Industries
PLC

SLTR-3/DOC9
EXTERNAL - TURN DOWN AFTER INTERVIEW

Your ref	Our ref	Tel ext		Date
————	————	————		——— ———

Dear

I am writing to inform you that, at present, we have no suitable positions vacant at Head Office.

As you will appreciate, we have many applications of high quality, like yours and a relatively small number of vacancies.

However, I would like to thank you for taking the time to visit Millbank more than once and for your interest in ICI.

We will keep your details on file, should anything suitable arise in the future. I hope this is not too much of a disappointment to you and hope you are successful in finding a suitable post elsewhere.

Yours sincerely

Personnel Officer
Head Office Personel Section

BIBLIOGRAPHY

Burston, Diane – *An A-Z of Careers and Jobs* (Kogan Page, 3rd edn., 1988, £6.95).

Donald, Vivien – *How to Choose a Career* (Kogan Page, 2nd edn., 1989, £4.95).

Janner, Greville – *Janner on Presentation* (Business Books, edn., 1986 £5.95).

Janner, Greville – *Janner's Complete Letterwriter* (Business Books, 3rd edn., 1989, £7.95).

Maitland, Iain – *How to Win at Interviews* (Business Books, 1989, £4.95).

Page, Anne – *Your First Job* (Kogan Page, 1983, £3.95).

Thompson, Mary – *Employment for Disabled People* (Kogan Page, 1986, £4.95).

Wallis, Margaret – *Getting There: Job Hunting for Women* (Kogan Page, 1987, £4.95).

Careers in . . . series (Kogan Page, pbk. £3.25–£3.95).

Jobs in . . . series (Kogan Page, pbk. £3.25).

INDEX

179